A Masterpiece on Suffering

Many books similar to *When Life Isn't Fair* have been written recently, but Freeman's work is especially noteworthy. Rather than easy, pat answers, Freeman offers solid biblical responses. And at each chapter's end he asks pointed questions that would help readers come to grips with their feelings and reflect on the truth of God's Word. In easy-to-understand terms, *When Life Isn't Fair* explains a profound theological mystery. After finishing this book, readers will have the courage to face life's seemingly unfair circumstances and to have faith in God's absolute wisdom and justice.

Bookstore Journal

When I became paralyzed in a diving accident, I felt that God owed me explanations. And my questions were not unlike those of most people who suffer hurt and disappointment. With wit and disarming style, Joel Freeman helps us find at least some of those answers.

Joni Eareckson Tada

In this helpful volume, Freeman combines compassion and tough-minded insight in his discussion of the age-old questions about evil and suffering. An honest reading of the book will dry some people's tears, and start some others!

Robert A. Cook, past president
National Religious Broadcasters

When Life Isn't Fair is one of the best commentaries to date on the heartaches, trials, and tribulations people experience during life's journey. What inspiration, comfort, and hope this blessed book should bring to multitudes who question God's sovereignty when depression, devastation, and death occur! As I dug deeper into this masterpiece on suffering, I saw it as a means of producing blessing, peace, and assurance to every intellectual level and age group.

Jack Van Impe

I have just concluded reading *When Life Isn't Fair*. It certainly was a pleasant experience. I found times when I wanted to laugh and also times when I felt like I really needed to cry. My congratulations to you on a fine piece of work.

Rex Humbard

Joel Freeman's acceptance and care speaks to the heart of many who search for meaning and purpose. In touch with human suffering and pain, his personal faith is witness to God's mercy and love. Freeman's moving message in the book *When Life Isn't Fair* is one of profound hope.

Barry K. Estadt, Ph.D.
Chairman, Loyola College
Pastoral Counseling Program

Why doesn't God abide by my personal standards of what's fair and what isn't? I discovered a most satisfying answer through the stories, humor, and good thinking of Joel Freeman.

David R. Mains
Chapel of the Air

I just got done reading your book *When Life Isn't Fair*. I wanted to tell you just how much I enjoyed your book. Of all the ones I've read, it has given me the most insight to suffering. The examples you give are excellent and hit home! The questions at the end of the chapters are very helpful to see how I feel. It is one of those books I will read again and again.

A satisfied reader
Austin, Texas

I have just finished your book *When Life Isn't Fair*, and honestly believe it is the best thing that has ever happened to me. I would have traded my entire life for this book 25 years ago.

A reflective prisoner
Vevay, Indiana

*W*HEN *L*IFE *I*SN'T *F*AIR

*M*AKING *S*ENSE *O*UT OF *S*UFFERING

*J*OEL *A*. *F*REEMAN, *P*H.*D*.

New Leaf Press

NEW LEAF PRESS

First printing: February 2002

Copyright © 2002 by Joel A. Freeman. All rights reserved. No part of this book may be used or reproduced in any manner whatsoever without written permission of the publisher except in the case of brief quotations in articles and reviews. For information write: New Leaf Press, Inc., P.O. Box 726, Green Forest, AR 72638.

ISBN: 0-89221-522-4
Library of Congress Number: 2001098910

Unless otherwise indicated, Scripture quotations are from the King James Version. Scripture quotations designated (GNB) are from the Good News Bible, and those designated (NIV) are from the New International Version.

The excerpt from the song "Sympathy for the Devil," written by Mick Jagger and Keith Richards, © 1968 by ABKCO Music, Inc., is used by permission. All rights reserved.

Unless specifically identified as factual, all names have been fictionalized for protection and privacy.

Printed in the United States of America.

Please visit our website for other great titles:
www.newleafpress.net

For information regarding author interviews, contact the publicity department at (870) 438-5288.

To Shirley,
my beloved wife
and best friend

CONTENTS

FOREWORD

As a Christian psychiatrist, I have counseled literally hundreds of men, women, and children who have been bitterly angry at God for being unfair. The basic reason is always the same: God, in His sovereignty, either allowed or caused something to happen to these people that they would not have allowed if they were in God's position. They are angry at God for not letting them be in absolute control. This attitude stems from the basic sin of arrogance and pride.

What really astounds me is that even though I consider myself an enlightened human being who meditates on God's Word daily, I also get angry with God from time to time for not running my life circumstances the way I would like. Because I am human I will always do this to some extent, but I have learned what to do when I develop this attitude of arrogance.

In this book, Joel Freeman does an excellent job of gently knocking the wind out of our arrogant "life isn't fair" sails. His personal vulnerability helps us to understand that we aren't unique in having these thoughts, and he gives us an uplifting glimpse of God's overall plan, showing us that our limited understanding insufficiently qualifies us for determining what is fair or unfair.

Paul Meier, M.D.
Co-founder and medical director of
New Life Clinics, Dallas, Texas

CHAPTER

- ONE -

WHY?

> All horrors have followed the same
> course, getting worse and forcing you into
> a kind of bottleneck till, at the very mo-
> ment when you thought you must be
> crushed, behold! You were out of the nar-
> rows and all was suddenly well. The ex-
> traction hurt more and more and then the
> tooth was out. The dream became a night-
> mare and then you awoke. You die and die
> and then you are beyond death.
>
> — C.S. Lewis

Why are there fleas? Have you ever asked that question? No? (Obviously you've never owned a cat or dog.)
Well, just think a°bout it. What purpose do they serve?
Granted, their existence creates the jobs necessary in
the conception, testing, manufacturing, and market-
ing of anti-flea shampoos and sprays. But why are they
here on this planet? They are dirty and nasty and they
reproduce at an incredible rate. Why did God deliberately create such seemingly unnecessary pests? Why
do they exist? Is there an answer?

In the same breath we could ask: Why is there
pain? You know, gut-wrenching grief and sorrow? Does

it have any meaning? Let's face it; life presents many challenges to all of us.

Some people piously portray emotional pain as a brilliant blessing in disguise that really is our best friend. Somehow, pain is supposed to be a useful tool, teaching us valuable lessons.

That philosophy seems rather hollow and empty, however, when talking with people who are in the throes of pain or who have endured hardship. What about the couple who loses their long-awaited newborn child three days after birth, or the woman who has discovered the ugly realities about her lingering, crippling disease, or the man with two kids who has lost his wife in a terrorist attack? What should we say when they ask, "Why is this happening to me?" Or how do we respond when they plead, "Please help me — how do I cope?"

A child is conceived in ecstasy, but birthed with much pain. The sharpest, hottest tears of a parent, however, are not caused by physical pain. They are the result of a sorrow that is more deeply rooted in the human soul than the body — the pain of a broken heart. And that is the way it is with life. Ideas and dreams are conceived with great enthusiasm, but the implementation of those concepts invites suffering and pain.

Some people are bombarded with heartache and tragedy, while others appear to navigate through life hardly touched by difficulty. Yet everyone endures emotional pain. Suffering is a universal language.

I know that language. Like many, I have felt my own emotional pain while crying out, "I never want to hurt this bad again." I have been through some tough stuff — some of it far too personal to include in a book.

On Friday, November 16, 2001, Shirley and I were awakened at 2 a.m. by the shrill ringing of the telephone. Nighttime phone calls usually mean trouble. And what we heard verified our suspicions. It was horrifying. Our 33-year-old nephew, Michael, had tragically careened off the road and was dead. We both were numb as we made our way in the chilly darkness across the street to the beautiful home he had built for his wife (30) and two children (ages 2 and 4). His wife was sobbing. As the morning progressed, whenever another family member arrived, a new wave of grief filled the living room. The next week was a blur. Visiting the accident site with his father and brother. The funeral. Weeping. Laughing at the memory of Michael's legendary youthful escapades. And then weeping some more.

As time has passed, I have become more aware of the excruciating physical pain Michael experienced for many years, the result of an inherited illness — ankylosing spondylitis, a severe type of rheumatoid arthritis. Eventually it would have fused his spine together, so that he would not be able to bend over.

Later his wife, Joy, showed me a letter that he had written to her about two years prior. Michael dealt with the mountains and valleys just like us all, but he never complained about his pain in my presence. That was the way he lived his life. The depth of his mental and physical agony is somewhat revealed in the following vignettes:

> Up until recently I have been able to paint on a smile and pretend that everything was fine. Over the past month or so, my facade has begun to crack. . . . I apologize for the times of venting, withdrawal, and

attitudes of gloom. . . . I hope that by reading this [letter] you will better understand
what is really going on in my mind. . . . My
worst struggles are when the symptoms
change. As I find myself not being able to
do the things I could do before, I get upset. My other concern is dignity. The
thought of asking for help with things I
could always do before is tough. There is
also my pride. People know something is
wrong with me but when they see me I
look normal. If somebody has a cast on
their foot, everybody understands and sym-
pathizes. But when people say sympathiz-
ing things to me, I feel kinda stupid or embarrassed. There is no proof. People might
think I'm just a big whiner. Very few people
truly understand what is wrong with me.
Most people think I just have a bad back,
but so does 2/3 of the USA. . . . My worst
fear is wondering if I can be a good dad.
The last few weeks I felt too bad to play
with the kids. I didn't even want to be there.
I just wanted to be left alone. "Leave me
alone, I don't feel good." Does that sound
like a good father? Justifiable or not, it's not
the way things should be. I'm getting desperate . . . our minds are more fragile than
we think. There are many well-docu-
mented cases of criminal suspects confess-
ing to crimes they never committed after
hours of relentless and suggestive police
questioning. People reach a point of des-

peration where they are willing to do anything to stop the inundation of negative
input to the brain . . . this unpredictable
random cycle of knee, back, and hip pain,
stomach cramps, stiffness, and fatigue is
driving me crazy. Every week it's something
new.

I had never before realized the full extent of how
remarkable a man Michael had been to his family,
friends, and associates. The perseverance and poise he
displayed was in spite of the continual "private hell"
he experienced in his knees, back, and hips. The shoot-
ing pain tested the outer limits of his endurance.

By the way, what is your "private hell"? It may be
something physical, mental, emotional, financial, rela-
tional, or spiritual — or a combination of all. For decades I have worked with many people of privilege,
including professional athletes, highly successful busi-
nessmen, and folks in the music/entertainment indus-
tries. I have also worked with many people who experience the dregs of humanity on a daily basis, at street
level. And many who experience life in between. Regardless of one's station in life, there is a drama of pain
behind every pair of eyes.

Over the years, I have become more understanding
of and patient with people who, like Michael, are overwhelmed by the pain, some even railing out against God
in the midst of personal trauma. You see, I too have
asked similar questions and made similar statements
when placed in the crucible of "unfair" circumstances.
When in those situations, I have been amazed by the
depths of rage I have been capable of experiencing.

The Holocaust in Nazi Germany is a constant re-minder of what lurks beneath the surface of people, even those immersed in education, science, and religion. What disturbs us the most, though, for the most part, is that the perpetrators looked so normal. Emotional pain forces all of us to confront that unpleasant stuff that lies just under the thin veneer of professionalism. Is that the primary task of pain? Maybe. Maybe not.

In the future chapters I will relate a limited picture of my own struggles and will share time-tested principles that have sustained me before, during, and after "unfair" events that have left my emotional system raw and bleeding — in a state of shock.

The "why" of suffering is the most potent assassin that haunts, taunts, and seeks to destroy the strong and the weak alike. Questions hit us all — those who are currently in the midst of suffering, those who are trying to assist in some way, and those who are in the people-helping profession, feeling empty and exhausted, needing to be recharged.

This book is not filled with glib answers, which serve to drive honest strugglers into deeper disillusionment. In fact, I am rather suspect of those who seem to have all the answers wrapped up in a neat, tidy package: Ten Principles for Happy Sufferers. Instead I want to hand you some tools. It will take longer, cost more, and be messier than previously anticipated — but well worth the upward, the inward, and the outward journey. I also want you to know that we are in this together. I am learning and growing right along with you.

Before you have finished reading, you will have discovered ways to improve your course in life by making your attitude behave. You will also understand how you have already won the invisible, spiritual battle being waged this very moment for the attention of your heart.

First, you are about to meet an unusual group of people in a rather unique drama. A place has been reserved for you.

PERSONAL REFLECTION OR DISCUSSION

1. Have you ever gone through a painful, hurtful experience that caused you to question the "fairness" of God? Think back on the specifics of the situation and try to remember what your innermost feelings were at that time.

2. Your past, present, and future "unfair" experiences are prime candidates for God's healing. As you read *When Life Isn't Fair*, ask Him to help you apply the principles you will be learning.

CHAPTER

- TWO -

COSMIC KILLJOY

> I still rebel and complain against God,
> I cannot keep from groaning. How I wish I
> knew where to find him, and knew how to
> go where he is. I would state my case be-
> fore him and present all the arguments in
> my favor. I want to know what he would
> say and how he would answer me (Job
> 23:1–5; GNB).

Picture this: A convocation of grumpy people are meeting on a hillside to have a gripe session with God. The
first person to make his case is Moses. He firmly grasps
his cane and takes an authoritative step forward. He
looks dramatically to his left. His gaze then sweeps to
the right. He pauses deliberately, stroking his flowing
beard. He looks directly at God, and booms in a
Charlton Heston-type voice, "God, we've known each
other quite well. You did a great job with the Red Sea
and Pharaoh's army. Really now, couldn't I have at least
taken one step into the land of Canaan? I have been
nursing a grudge against You for a few thousand years.
I must get something off my chest. My experience with
You hasn't been totally pleasant. You deliberately built

me up, just to let me down. All I did was hit the rock! What's the big deal?

"Hey listen," Moses continues with his voice rising in emotion, "I gave up the comforts of Egypt as Pharaoh's number-two man. I followed You without question. All I got in return was 40 years on the back side of a lousy desert, 40 additional years of dealing with a multitude of people who behaved like thankless morons, and then I died just 30 days before everybody else went into the Promised Land! I'm disgusted with You. You're simply not 'fair'!"

God smiles reverently and silently nods to the next in line.

John the Baptist clears his throat, nervously looking at a crumpled piece of paper clutched in his hand. He begins, "God, I know You are righteous and holy, but I am really annoyed with You. The more I think about it, the madder I get. Let me ask You a question: Have You ever had to eat grasshoppers? I had to — YUK! Furthermore, You commanded me to trudge over hill and dale, yelling about repentance at the top of my lungs. That's not all! After working so hard for You, I ended up in a prison cell and then unceremoniously got my head lopped off! It just isn't 'fair'! I believe You exploited me for Your personal gain. Is that the way You operate? Do You enjoy squeezing people for all You can get out of them and then delight in spitting them out? Huh? Is that what You do?"

God smiles disarmingly and nods to another individual. This one carries himself with an aristocrat's bearing. His name is Job. He brushes his nose with his finger and speaks. "God, I know You have almost everything under control. But, I believe You are a 'cosmic killjoy.'

You must sit on Your throne, waiting until someone is enjoying life to the fullest. Then, You must break into sinister laughter and wring Your hands gleefully. I can see it clearly; then what You do is smash everything that person owns. Don't try to back out of this one; I'm here personally to attest to the fact that this is a favorite pastime of Yours."

At this point, everyone nods vigorously and grunts affirmatively.

Job continues, "I was a helpless victim. Without consulting me, You gave the devil permission to rip me apart. I lost 7,000 sheep, 3,000 camels, my oxen, donkeys, servants, seven sons, and my three precious daughters. That's not all; while I was sitting in the ashes of my burned-out house, nursing my boils, my wife told me that I had lost my integrity, and that I should curse You and die. God, I don't even begin to understand why this happened to me. You are 'unfair' in Your dealings, not only with me, but with every person who walks on the face of the earth!"

As God looks down the line, He sees many people whose tempers are rising. John is complaining about his "Social Security benefits" on the insane-asylum island called Patmos. The other disciples are griping about their disconcerting experiences with martyrdom. Jeremiah complains about the dungeon conditions where he had mud practically up to his ears.

Paul has a long list to grumble about: He was shipwrecked three times, naked, hungry, bitterly persecuted, stoned, rejected by the religious system, jailed, and finally killed. Joseph is steaming mad because he was sold as a slave, framed by the boss's wife, and thrown in jail. His only crime was a dream! Honest, pure

Stephen still has lumps and bruises from being stoned to death.

Also, God can't overlook David. Jealous Saul hunted him like an animal. Then, after 30 minutes of sin with Bathsheba, David reaped literal havoc within his family and kingdom for 40 years. Each one has a briefcase full of "facts" that justify his primary complaint: God is not "fair."

As I depict the preceding scene, I do so with my tongue firmly planted in my cheek. But I am completely serious about this one point: Every human, at one time or another, asks the following 60-million-dollar questions — "If God is a God of love, why is there so much suffering in the world? Why do the wicked seem to prosper? Why do terrible things happen to nice people? Why does life have to hurt so much? Isn't there an easier way to grow? Can any meaning be found in suffering?"

There are no glib answers to these universal questions. In fact, volumes have been written in an effort to address each question specifically. Many of these books assist in providing a measure of comfort to those in the midst of gut-wrenching trials.

I will not attempt to provide generic-brand solutions to problems that have vexed thinkers for centuries. In his booklet *Why Does God Allow Suffering?* Paul Malte explains:

> The Bible itself never offers very easy answers to suffering, or to sufferers. Even in Job, the classic book on suffering, the problem of evil is never explained away. But, Job does learn to live with suffering — and with the Lord Creator. Deep in his soul —

not his mind — Job discovers the peace, which transcends all human understanding. Jesus — who claims to be God's representative among men — never unties the intellectual problem of God's goodness and God's power. He simply acts to demonstrate the Father's goodness and His power channeled personally to people. Jesus does not heal all the lepers in Palestine, exorcise all unclean spirits, and make whole all marriages. Wherever and whenever He can, He heals and He helps. He gives people the inner attitude, the courage, and the joy, to handle suffering. He does nothing to ward off His own death, and He becomes the victim of human hostility. He suffers both the anguish of physical death and the hell of alienation from God. By suffering with us He suffers for us. He suffers so that our suffering might be transformed and transcended into triumph.

Christians have no tidy answers to suffering, no easy ten principles for happy suffers. They only have attitudes for meeting it, handles for overcoming it, outlooks for transcending it.[1]

A major blockage to enjoying life to the fullest is the "fairness" question. The "fairness" issue has invaded every home. You know the scene — little Mary comes running into the house at curfew, and says, "How come Johnny gets to stay outside for another hour? Why do I have to go to bed? Mom, you're not 'fair'!"

Our children can't see the bigger picture. When they get married and have children of their own, they soon understand some of the reasons for their parents' "because I-told-you-so" decisions. They eventually realize that love motivates parents to make choices that aren't always consistent with the wishes and timing of children.

No two children are created with equal talents, mental capacities, or physical opportunities. Sibling rivalry can develop when a younger child follows an athletic big brother or popular big sister in school. It is not "fair" when they are constantly referred to as "Jim's younger brother" or "Mary's little sister." Friction can also result when a child of a large family consumes 60 percent of the household income because of a periodic illness. It's not "fair" when the sickness of one child governs the lifestyle of the entire family.

Every soccer field and Little League diamond has hosted angry parents who are disgruntled with their children's lack of playing time. These parents exhibit unhealthy role models in front of their children. The theme of "fairness" characterizes their attitudes as they second guess the coach's decisions and grumble about the performance of the one who played in their child's stead.

Grades, special privileges, and difficult tasks provide many opportunities for students to harp upon the theme of "fairness" in the classroom setting. Many a harried teacher has spent agonizing moments questioning his or her ability after an intense case of verbal assault and battery from a rebellious student or reactionary parent.

Alone in his office, a businessman buries his face

in his hands, frustrated over the loss of a large business deal that was won by a competitor through unethical means. He doesn't mind losing an account, but not as a result of unscrupulous business practices. It's not "fair."

Every pastor who is worth his salt has struggled with God's apparent lack of "fairness." Undue criticism and pressure are a part of the real estate when one enters into a position of leadership. The pastor who knows what it's like to draw up into a fetal position on the floor and sob until there are no tears left is a man who can be mightily used by God if he dares to settle the "fairness" question.

At best, a marriage will suffer from peaceful coexistence if the "fairness" issues are not squarely confronted in both lives. In recent decades, the divorce rate has skyrocketed because, by and large, individuals have decided that personal pleasure and convenience take precedence over commitment.

The pathways to alcoholism and drug addiction are paved with the "fairness" problem. Addicts feel that since life has dealt them a dirty deal they have the right to drown, smoke, or snort their sorrows into oblivion.

Every church has experienced the ruckus caused by some disgruntled pew-warmer. Or, what about the crabby deacon? What about the church split that was caused by a difference of opinion over the carpet color in the sanctuary? The group that vacated the premises claimed it wasn't "fair."

People who are single by choice, divorce, or death must grapple with the theme of "fairness." But they are not the only ones who fight the "fairness" question. What about the terminally ill, the handicapped, the children of divorced parents, or the abused spouses?

Does the cheater get the highest grade? Does the liar get elected to office? Does the embezzler live in the mansion on the hill? Is God a "cosmic killjoy," as some would have us believe?

"Fair" is a fine word, but as you will see, the genuine meaning has been distorted. To help clarify its meaning, the word "fair" is set off by quotation marks throughout the book. By the way, how did the "fairness" concept start?

PERSONAL REFLECTION OR DISCUSSION

1. In your opinion, is God "fair"?

2. The hypothetical gripe session with God was attended by Moses, John the Baptist, Job, Paul, John, Jeremiah, Stephen, and David. Which biblical character do you identify with most when it comes to questioning God's "fairness"?

3. Do you recall any instances in your life when you realized that God has been more than just "with you"?

4. What is your yardstick of "fairness"? In relation to what?

There is only one being who can satisfy the last aching abyss of the human heart, and that is the Lord Jesus Christ.

(Oswald Chambers 1874–1917)

CHAPTER

- THREE -

SYMPATHY FOR THE DEVIL

Adversity does not make us frail; it only shows us how frail we are.

— Abraham Lincoln

Have you ever felt sorry for the devil? Maybe just a twinge of pity? After all, he was kicked out of heaven without a second chance. Isn't it true that God was abrupt and unkind in the way He handled Satan?

Without a moment's hesitation, you probably answered the preceding questions with a resounding No! It didn't take long for you to respond. As an intelligent being, Satan knows that most people aren't inclined to fill their crying towels with tears because of his awful plight as the fallen prince of darkness.

Most people understand that Lucifer became overly conscious of his beauty in heaven and his value to God. Many are aware that pride motivated him to make the grandiose statement found in Isaiah 14:13–14: "I will ascend to heaven and rule the angels. I will take the highest throne. I will preside on the mount of Assembly far away in the north. I will climb to the highest heavens. I will be like the Most High."

Almost everyone has read that God, refusing to coexist with this haughty being, gave him the left foot of fellowship. As a result, BAM!, Satan was booted out of heaven like a bolt of lightning. But he didn't leave alone; one-third of all the angels in heaven impudently acknowledged their independence of God and followed close on Lucifer's heels.

Ever since that event in history, Satan has been boiling mad and is driven to influence humans into thinking God is not "fair" in His dealings. This is all part of his massive public relations campaign, which is designed to turn creatures against their Creator.

Satan unveiled his strategy in the Garden of Eden. In fact, the unabridged edition of the "Freeman Translation" quotes Lucifer as saying, "Eve, you mean to tell me that God told you not to eat of the 'no-no' fruit? Oh, that's terrible! You must feel so rejected. I can understand how you feel. I have had a lot of personal experience with God. He has a huge ego — He's only interested in a one-man show. He really isn't 'fair.' He is threatened by anyone who might become His equal. He probably doesn't want you to eat the fruit because of how much you'll know after the first bite. He wants to hold you back from advancement, thereby cramping your style forever. Go ahead, take a bite. You'll be enlightened with a new level of consciousness. That's it — just one teensy-weensy, itsy-bitsy bite. . . ."

Now that you know the scoop about what really went on in the Garden of Eden, it is easy to comprehend the devil's strategy in the here and now. Through precise maneuvers by his invisible host of demons, he waits until people are in a vulnerable state of mind, and then he hits them between the eyes with timeless reminders like:

- God has forgotten and forsaken you.
- God doesn't love you as much as He loves other people.
- God is a hard, cruel taskmaster.
- You have committed the unpardonable sin.
- You wouldn't be hurting so badly if God had everything under control.
- God is not "fair."

Lucifer wants to take advantage of every opportunity to attack his former boss. He slanders and curses Him at every turn, maliciously hoping to build his success by trying to defeat Christ. His evil thoughts against God are blatantly exposed in the following statements:

> I dip my forefinger in the watery blood of your impotent, mad redeemer and write over his thorn-torn brow: The true prince of evil — the king of slaves.
>
> I gaze into the glassy eye of your fearsome Jehovah and pluck him by the beard; I lift a broadax and split open his worm-eaten skull!
>
> Behold the crucifix: what does it symbolize? Pallid incompetence hanging on a tree. . . .
>
> He who turns the other cheek is a cowardly dog! Self-preservation is the highest law.
>
> Life is the great indulgence — death, the great abstinence. Therefore, make the most of life here and now.
>
> Say to thine own heart, "I am my own redeemer."[1]
>
> — The Satanic Bible

One can clearly see that Satan is not operating under the guise of a hidden agenda. He absolutely despises Jesus Christ and will seek to destroy anyone who confesses Him as his or her Savior and Lord.

Recently, I was reintroduced to the reality of Satan's ongoing plan to sabotage God's character by promoting the "fairness" concept to humans. While driving across town to visit friends one rainy evening, the soaked form of a hitchhiker suddenly appeared in the beam of my headlight. Being a former hitchhiker, I instinctively screeched to a halt. A young man in his early twenties climbed in, thanking me profusely. His smile was framed by rather long, damp hair. We proceeded on our way, introducing ourselves and exchanging a few pleasantries. Taking advantage of the opportunity to talk with him about Jesus, I waited for a few moments and then nonchalantly inquired, "Fred, are you interested in spiritual things?"

I was not prepared for his answer. In an even tone, he informed me, "Yeah, I am. I've been studying the occult for several years now." Intrigued, I feigned naiveté by asking him questions that gently probed the depth of his involvement. At first he answered in a guarded manner, but then he began to share more freely. I soon discovered the seriousness of his dedication to the devil's cause.

As we drove on, I asked Fred to explain the circumstances that led up to and followed Lucifer's grand exit from heaven. Without hesitation, he graphically described God's injustice in dealing with Satan. He went on to explain that Satan had a legitimate gripe against a God who was jealous, cruel, and "unfair" in the way He had handled the devil.

As we conversed, two predominant thoughts entered my mind. I remembered an event that occurred on a Thursday evening in 1974, an event so significant that it is indelibly etched in my memory.

As a group of fervent Bible college students, we were gathered for an evening of theological discussion and prayer. About 50 people were present. Suddenly the evening was shattered by the actions and utterances of a woman who had come to visit the school for a week.

I am very cautious about attributing abnormal human behavior to satanic activity, but this woman's words and actions were indicative of demonic possession. At one point she reacted violently — kicking, cursing, and biting. At times she had to be restrained by two muscular men.

"You all think you're so smart," she screamed in an unearthly voice. "Well, I want you to know that we are more powerful. We are winning. We have control over the whole world." A cold, involuntary shiver pulsated up and down my spine as the reality of kingdom warfare hit me full in the face.

Her darkened eyes narrowed as she dramatically surveyed everyone in the room. For a brief, eternal moment our eyes locked and then disengaged. She proudly tossed her head, clearing the black, bushy hair from the sides of her sweaty face and seethed, "I hate every one of you. I hate you all."

As the night wore on, she spoke in several different voices on everything from drugs to the subject of "666," the mark of the beast. Sometimes her words came in guttural tones, others in soft and mellow voices, while others were punctuated with a combination of high-pitched shrieks.

One statement, however, penetrated my memory on this rainy evening in the car with the hitchhiker. One of her utterances had come in a pitifully haunting voice: "It is not 'fair.' You get many chances, but we got only one chance."*

As I drove through the rain I also remembered the title of a rock song popularized by a musical group called the Rolling Stones. The reality of the title of the song, "Sympathy for the Devil," had a chilling effect on me. As we continued our ride, I was able to recall some of its lyrics:

> Please allow me to introduce myself:
> I'm a man of wealth of taste.
> I've been around for long, long years —
> Stolen many a man's soul and faith.
> I was around when Jesus Christ
> Had His moment of doubt and faith.
> I made damn sure that Pilate
> Washed his hands, and sealed his fate.
>
> Pleased to meet you,
> Hoped you guessed my name.
> But what's puzzling you
> Is the nature of my game.

* Author's Note: In my opinion, this incident was an actual case of demon possession. The majority of cases, however, that involve individuals having bizarre psychotic breaks with reality, may actually be people suffering from a dopamine imbalance in the brain. They may hear voices or even experience visual hallucinations. Many times this is correctable by proper doses of Thorazine. A Christian psychiatrist should be consulted.

Just as every cop is a criminal
And all the sinners, Saints
As heads is tails, just call me Lucifer
'Cause I'm in need of some courtesy
Have some sympathy and some taste.
Use all your well-learned politesse
Or I'll lay your soul to waste![2]

As I reflected on these thoughts, Satan's strategy became much clearer. With each passing moment, Fred was verifying my suspicions as he tried to impress me as to why Satan had received the raw end of the deal. We were just warming up to the subject at hand when he suddenly interjected, "I've got to get off at this next exit."[3]

In the darkness, I fumbled around in the pouch under the driver's seat and hastily pulled out a gospel tract, handing it to him. "Fred, I'm interested in your thoughts about God and Satan," I said. "Your comments tonight show that you have been thinking deeply about spiritual matters. Please accept this piece of paper from me. It will explain God's power to forgive your sins and give you a brand-new perspective about life."

I pulled the car over just after the exit ramp and asked him to have an "Elijah Showdown."

"What's that?" he quizzed, laughing slightly, with his hand on the door handle.

"Well, Fred," I continued, "there's a story in the Bible about the prophet Elijah who bragged that his God was true and that the god Baal was false. Elijah then proposed that two altars be built on top of a mountain and that the real God would pour fire down from the sky. The prophets of Baal took him up on the challenge, with thousands of people gathered around waiting for the fireworks."

Knowing that I had a limited amount of time, I paused momentarily to see if he was still interested or if I was boring him to tears. Sensing perhaps what I was doing, Fred took his hand off the door handle and responded, "Go on. Then what happened?"

"Well, the prophets of Baal danced around for hours and nothing happened." With his expressed interest, I slowed down a bit. "When Elijah prayed, fire instantly came down and God showed that He was the only true God. Fred," I said softly, "God wants to prove to you that He is still the only true God. Satan is real and he has a lot of power, as you well know. But he has fed you a bunch of lies about what happened way back when he was kicked out of heaven. God is more powerful. Don't just take my word for it. Prove it for yourself by asking Jesus to come into your life and be your personal Savior. His blood was poured out on the Cross so that people like you and me can receive the free gift of eternal life. I'd like to see you come on the winning side."

There was an odd silence. And then he commented, "Thanks. You've given me a lot to think about." He paused again for a few seconds, opened the door and then turned to me, saying, "Thanks for the ride."

I sped off into the rainy night, hoping that somehow our conversation had made an impact on Fred's life. I know it did on mine.

Just like Fred, King David's friend Asaph swallowed the "fairness" concept — hook, line, and sinker. Asaph began to think that God was unjust in His dealings with people. In Psalm 73, Asaph compared his life with that of the wicked. According to his evaluation, the unrighteous enjoyed their lives to the fullest. They conducted unprincipled business practices and unabashedly flaunted their evil lifestyles, yet they had no glaring problems. They were so fat and prosperous that their eyes almost popped out of their sockets.

Asaph was almost sucked into Satan's "bad attitude" strategy against God until he went into the sanctuary and saw objective truth as it really was. He had become contaminated by worldly thinking and had compared his situation with the lifestyles of others. Up to this point, he didn't see the bigger picture of eternal value. But in the sanctuary, his mind became clear, and he could say, "There's none on earth I desire besides Thee, O Lord" (Ps. 73:25).

Knowing full well that the "fairness" theme was prevalent, the apostle Paul was careful to address the issue when talking about Jacob and Esau in Romans 9. Many scholars speculate regarding the reasons why God loved Jacob but hated Esau. Paul simply asked, "Is there unrighteousness [injustice] with God?" (Rom. 9:14). His take-it-or-leave-it answer was, "God forbid" — or in modern-day English, "No way!"

I am not a foaming-at-the-mouth, witch-hunting, there's-a-devil-in-your-closet demon chaser. But I am absolutely convinced of the fact that Satan has an organized host of commanding and commissioned officers. These foul spirits are united by the distorted belief that they can destroy the kingdom of God.

God deals with the devil somewhat like Uncle Bob plays a Thanksgiving Day football game with a child. (Everybody knows an Uncle Bob.) He takes his nephew out in the backyard, marks off the boundaries, and they proceed with the game. After scoring several touch-

SYMPATHY FOR THE DEVIL

downs, the child jumps up and down gleefully proclaiming, "I'm winning! I'm winning!"

Uncle Bob feigns a look of consternation and playfully responds with an "I'm-not-letting-that-happen-again-you-little-stinker" vow. The friends and relatives watching are thoroughly enjoying the spectacle without experiencing one bit of fear for Uncle Bob and his lack of control or ability to win. They know what Uncle Bob knows: Even if the score is 236-0 in favor of the kid, Uncle Bob can win any time he pleases. That knowledge permits Uncle Bob to be confident, actually exuberant, even in the midst of apparent defeat. So it is with God.

It may sound strange, but Satan's desire is to get human beings to feel sorry for him as the underdog in his "football game" against God. Granted, it's a tough assignment for the public relations department in hell, but the way he is trying to accomplish this mammoth task is by amplifying God's apparent lack of "fairness" when earth-shaking events occur on a personal basis or on a worldwide scale.

The automatic result is that our childlike trust in God's character as the sovereign ruler of the universe is at best eroded, or at worst, smashed. We become disillusioned with God and then we enter into a phase whereby we frantically search for happiness without consulting God's guidance. Of course, our search for happiness does not produce the desired results, so our disillusionment with God and the people who follow Him intensifies.

Over a period of time, Satan capitalizes on our natural bent toward rationalization and bitterness, and we end up with a mere plastic shell of religion that lacks substance and power. Slowly but surely, our understanding becomes darkened, and we fall prey to man-centered ideals that leave God totally out of the picture. We are now available to accept any form of deception as truth because something is missing.

PERSONAL REFLECTION OR DISCUSSION

1. As you look back on your life, think of two situations in the past two years where Satan tried to convince you that God was "unfair" during those times. Have developments since then caused you to modify your attitudes at all?

2. In retrospect, can you identify at least one positive attribute in your life that God has developed through those unpleasant experiences?

3. According to Romans 5:1–5, why do you think God allows hardship into a person's life?

CHAPTER

- FOUR -

ADJUST TO THE JUSTICE OF GOD

> Injustice is relatively easy to bear; what
> stings is justice. — H.L. Mencken

At this moment I can hear someone in the middle of a swamp, up to his tail in alligators, yelling, "Hey, wait a minute! How does the 'fairness' issue affect me, and how can I avoid being a sucker for the devil's tactics?" I'm so glad he asked.

Most people are bona fide, card-carrying members of the Navel Gazing Society (N.G.S.). You haven't heard of it? I'm surprised. Pause momentarily and think about the last time you made an utter fool of yourself. Maybe you inadvertently opened your mouth and blabbed some stupid comment in the presence of important guests.

Did you feel a sudden rush of embarrassment? Later that evening, did you toss to and fro in bed as the little theater in your brain played the disgusting scene over and over again? Did you cry yourself to sleep? Was the following week wrecked because of periodic preoccupation with that particular upsetting event?

The more you analyzed, the deeper you went into

depression. You may have been able to explain the psychological ramifications brilliantly, but you couldn't seem to step out of the vicious cycle. As a long-lasting, distinguished member of N.G.S., I can understand. You see, I too, have suffered from the paralysis of self-analysis.

As I sit here at my writing desk reminiscing over some awkward, uncomfortable moments, I feel the flush of slight embarrassment. What about the time I preached a whole sermon and, well, I'd rather not say where, but a zipper that was supposed to be closed was . . . um, open? And the message was so good! What about the time I told a bald-headed joke to a bald-headed man? He tried to strangle me — well, almost. Or the time I went to the hospital, visiting a young boy who had just undergone an operation on his appendix and when I left, without thinking, I affectionately patted his stomach while saying goodbye, causing him to double over with a painful howl? His mother's smile of gratitude for my visit turned into a look of horror and panic.

Each time, I suffered for weeks as an official member of N.G.S., being overwhelmed periodically with depression and extreme self-consciousness at the mere thought of the disconcerting events. It wasn't until much later that the seriousness of the situations abated and a glimmer of humor slipped in with a degree of objectivity.

Something that has never ceased to amaze me, though, is how sudden situations give rise to instant feelings of anger, inferiority, retaliation, and self-justification. These feelings may have been masked in a pressure-free, predictable environment, but given the unexpected, we impulsively are at the mercy of the spasmodic reactions of our emotions.

First the bad news. Our hearts are deceitful and desperately wicked. God knows it, the Bible says it, and we profess it. But we are greatly surprised when the condition of our heart is exposed in unexpected situations. These are sovereignly designed circumstances that don't afford us the luxury of a pre-planned response. We react foolishly and then spend hours beating ourselves up, wondering why we allowed ourselves to go out of control. The answer is simple. Careful self-analysis may offer a more detailed explanation, but when all the smoke finally clears, we see that disguised selfishness and pride were the causes of our reaction.

The greater the trial, the more intense the pain. The greater the pain, the more we tend to question God's purpose. God, however, doesn't fall off His throne in utter shock when we yell at Him. He can handle abusive language and any number of fists shaken menacingly in His direction. He understands, and patiently waits until we have exhausted our show of bravado. He is not threatened, but He is not detached. His caring attitude does not change. He realizes that the heavenly complaint department will always be full of angry callers screaming, "God is not 'fair'!"

I was on that line years ago, yelling at God between sobs. Devastating news had broken my 19-year-old heart. The message was clear. In no uncertain terms, my girlfriend had said, "Joel, you're going to make a fine husband for some woman, but I'm not that woman." She had communicated it nicely and firmly, but all I could hear between her careful words was, "Beat it. Scram. Get out of my life, you no-good piece of junk. Consider yourself rejected. You are worthless. Do yourself a favor — go play in the traffic!"

In that moment of truth, I was frantic, searching madly for some reason and logic in it all. Nothing could console me. My best friends couldn't help. Everything was hopeless. I felt like a helpless little puppy, numb after a severe beating.

As humans, we are fragile creatures — always one hair's breadth away from insanity. Yet at the same time it is a paradox, because we are a stubborn, rebellious lot. Each new level of growth seems to be accompanied by much weeping and gnashing of teeth. We artfully plant our heels in the dirt, trying desperately to maintain the comfort zones we have so diligently established. At such times God brings in the demolition experts. He permits certain trials that gently blast us into the next spiritual zip code. We despise these afflictions and view them as nasty, uncalled-for pests (like fleas), but much later we say, "You know what? I now think I can understand why that had to happen. It was necessary, and above all it was good for me. I'm much better because of it."

"Hey, where's the good news?" I can hear our swampy piece of alligator bait ask. Hold on just a minute. Before continuing, we must understand a fundamental principle: God is in control. Absolutely nothing can happen to us or to anyone else without His consent. Even the devil has to check with God before he can cause disease, separation, or destruction. (As he did in the case of Job, for example.) Satan doesn't like the rules of this game. In his opinion, the rules are not "fair" because they are not in his favor.

Do you think Satan and his demons are depressed about what Christ did on Calvary? Of course they are! After all, Jesus defeated the works of the devil. Through

His blood, the Father now accepts us. Misery loves company. If we buy into it, Satan will cause us to feel exactly what he feels, think what he thinks, and say what he says about God's lack of "fairness."

"Fairness" reduces God's standards to the place where we can perform and function in life without utter, total dependence on Him. Complicating matters, "fairness" demands that we take time to clarify and evaluate circumstances from the limited perspective of each person involved, rather than from God's eternal viewpoint. As a direct product of humanistic philosophy, the "fairness" doctrine is based on man's value system and timetable. "Fairness" causes us to gaze at our navels and evaluate others from a subjective perspective. "Fairness" is incubated in hell.

The elder son's attitude illustrates the "fairness" focus in the story that Jesus told, commonly known as the Parable of the Prodigal Son (Luke 15:11–32). As the son walked in from another hard day of work in the field, he heard some festive music and observed some rather energetic dancing. Upon closer inspection, he discovered that all this merriment was in honor of his wayward younger brother's return from a distant country, where he had lived a life filled with wine, women, and song.

In so many words, he said, "Hey, this isn't 'fair'! All these years I've lived in the straight and narrow way. I've always been punctual and I've always been an honest worker, with a good, clean life. Yet, a party has never been thrown for me! My kid brother acts like a fool, runs away from home, and spends his entire inheritance. When he returns home, Dad empties the bank account to give him the royal treatment.

What's a guy gotta do to get some attention around here? Act crazy? Be honest with me. Does this look 'fair' to you?"

Since God isn't "fair" as humans perceive "fairness," what is the alternative? Could we please have a drum roll? Now for the good news: God is actually merciful and just. Satan does not want us to understand and apply this truth in everyday life. God is eternally motivated by justice. Regardless of how rampant sin is on the earth, God's justice prevails. The principles of justice are universal, being the same in the center of a busy marketplace in Shanghai as they are in the darkest corner of New York City. His justice is not optional and knows no time boundaries. And since God has the first and last word as the King of kings and Lord of lords, human beings who choose not to follow the precepts of His justice fall into deep trouble. Some may seem to escape the consequences while on earth, but will stand naked before Him at the judgment seat of Christ. There, all the hidden things of the heart will be pulled out from the shadows of human reasons and excuses. His truth prevails. Nothing escapes the ultimate justice of God.

God perfectly knows everything. He knows the focused direction of the heart of every person who has ever lived on this ancient spaceship called earth. He sees everything. He shows no favoritism. Justice reveals God's true nature of love and, at the same time, reveals the rebellious nature of man, which is placed on exhibit. Therefore, like an x-ray, justice establishes guilt when God's standards in His Word are violated. What are we to do?

PERSONAL REFLECTION OR DISCUSSION

1. What is the basic difference between "fairness" and justice?

2. In what ways could you adjust to God's sovereignty if your spouse or best friend died suddenly in an automobile accident?

3. How teachable are you?

CHAPTER

- FIVE -

ANGER AND FLEXIBILITY

> When life knocks you to your knees,
> stay there and fight. — Anonymous

I'm not angry. I'm just disappointed." Ever said something like that? The chameleon quality of anger makes it take on different forms – guilt, shame, cynicism, legalism, perfectionism, compulsions, pretense, and full-blown rage. Anger is so hard to pin down. Kind of like trying to wrestle smoke. This is true, especially in the grieving process. As humans we have a hard time understanding all this mercy and justice stuff. Perhaps it's because we have such a hard time understanding the big picture of anger and how it is expressed, especially by God.

Recently, I encountered an example of the nature of God's justice while studying a few verses in the ever-intriguing Book of Revelation. I had always believed that God poured out His anger on habitually wicked people only after His temper rose to the boiling point. It was then, I had believed, that God unleashed His rage upon arrogant sinners when He could tolerate the pressure no longer. "Okay, I've had enough. I'm going to let you have it!" Was I in for a surprise! King Jimmy calls it wrath, so let's refer to a few of the verses that exhibit the wrath of God during the Tribulation period.

> And the kings of the earth . . . said to the mountains and rocks, Fall on us, and hide us from the face of Him that sitteth on the throne, and from the wrath [*orge*] of the Lamb: For the great day of His wrath [*orge*] is come; and who shall be able to stand? (Rev. 6:15–17).

I better understood God's justice upon the discovery of two main words in the original Greek language that are translated "wrath" in the Book of Revelation. The word *thumos*[1] indicates a turbulent outburst of hot wrath, which erupts from an inward indignation. This word emphasizes a boiling agitation or commotion that is subject to sudden rises in emotion. It can be used to describe an individual who is usually considerate, but when given a certain set of upsetting circumstances can lose his or her temper in an explosive manner.

The other term of significance that is translated "wrath" in Revelation is *orge*[2], which denotes wrath in the sense of anger and vengeance. This suggests more of an abiding, settled attitude. In summary, *thumos* is the boiling agitation of the emotions while *orge* is a settled habit of mind.

In the Book of Revelation, *orge* is always indicated when God's wrath is mentioned. This reveals an important aspect about the implementation of His justice in the way He deals with His created beings. He has always retained and will always retain a settled hatred against sin, coupled with a permanent love for righteousness.

In other words, God does not "lose His temper." Nor does He take vengeance in an unjust, knee-jerk manner. God's hatred of wickedness has always been eternally present in His nature. During the Tribulation period He still maintains the same settled attitude regarding sin and righteousness that He has retained throughout each event in human history, including the way in which He dealt with Lucifer before his fall from heaven. He functions objectively, which enables Him to cause the sun to rise on the evil and the good each day and to send the much-needed rain for the crops of the righteous and unrighteous (Matt. 5:45).

No appeals mixed with "fairness" logic will change His mindset. His justice stands, regardless of the situational ethics or extenuating circumstances. "Fairness" tries to remove guilt, usually by mocking principles set forth in God's Word or by shifting the blame. ("I act the way I do because my mother forced me to eat porridge when I was a kid.") Justice, however, states that we are individually responsible for our internal attitudes and external behavior. Taking responsibility is the first giant step toward mental, emotional, and spiritual health. Justice by itself would send us all to hell. How about it — do you want to demand justice in your "unfair" situation?

This is where mercy comes riding in as our knight in shining armor. Through the eyes of mercy, He looks beyond our faults and sees our needs, patiently viewing us as finished products — even while we are in process. I respect His justice from a distance, but I wallow in His mercy up close and personal. Mercy is given to those who agree with God's standards of righteousness, but then immediately confess their inability to achieve those standards. This, however, requires adjustments on our part.

As an avid downhill skier, I have been following the latest technology in ski bindings. On an average run, skis undergo a tremendous amount of flex. Obviously, this causes the bindings to alternately separate slightly and then press hard against the soles of the boots, depending upon the position of the skis. Within recent decades, bindings have been designed to adjust with the skis so that the same pressure is always applied against the boots, thereby ensuring greater safety for the bones of the skier.

This exemplifies a truth about us. Romans 12:2 claims that we are continually transformed when our minds spiritually adjust to God's way of thinking in the midst of extreme pressure: A home burns down. Disillusionment strikes because of an unfulfilled desire. Personal failure invites one into the paralysis of analysis. A prisoner is denied parole. A loved one finds that he or she is in the advanced stages of an incurable disease. A bright young man is accidentally hit by a car and is paralyzed from the neck down. A top executive has a heart attack. A teenage son or daughter is arrogantly rebellious. A wife discovers her husband has been unfaithful. One's finances are out of control. A woman has been raped. You fill in the blanks.

In any of these moments of severe flexion we have options:

1. go crazy;
2. commit suicide;
3. adjust to God's way of thinking.

These are all real-life situations that smash us to the ground as crumpled forms of humanity. At first we are shocked. We deny it has happened to us. We weep until we experience "dry heaves." Motivated by anger, we then strike out at the ones we love the most, frantically searching for meaning in our pain. When all natural strength is abated, somehow we are ushered into the awesome presence of God where the resources for creative suffering are offered to us. There is a gentle, sweet communication with Him. Struggle ceases; we accept our suffering as God's gift to us. Bending beyond imagination, but not destroyed. An introduction to flexibility under pressure. It is here that we choose not to waste our sorrows.

What has happened is that we have adjusted to the justice of God. We have entered into a new phase of fellowship with Him. Does it always have to happen this dramatically? No, but many times it does. Perhaps it depends upon how deeply God has chosen to cut into the core of our hearts. It has been said that God does not look for medals, degrees, or diplomas. He looks for scars.

But how do we handle the flex, adjusting to His justice? In a later chapter we will discover how Job settled the "fairness" question and adjusted to God's mercy and justice, but I'll give you a sneak preview. After Job was confronted with the great power of God, he realized how small he and his problems were. He immediately was made painfully aware of his dire need for God's mercy.

God did not specifically answer his former questions about God's "fairness." Rather, Job was overwhelmed by the revelation of God's presence. Automatically, questions were no longer a big deal for Job and he adjusted to God's justice. Nothing changed except Job's mind. In the end, he had no problems extending mercy to his three judgmental buddies, and God gave him a double blessing.

In the midst of pain, our emotions run wild. That is why we desperately need a crash diet of objective assistance from the Scriptures. Here in the 21st century, we adjust to the justice of God by having a categorical understanding about God. It is also important for us to understand His intentions for us because when we are hurting, we generally put His motives on trial and question His integrity.

Some may say, "God is so mysterious, no one can really know who He is!" While it is true that God is so great that no human thought can fully contain Him, we do have the ability to know God. Our responsibility is to pump the knowledge we do have about God into our minds and then ask the Holy Spirit to make it a reality in good times as well as bad.

The following attributes of God are primed and ready to be pumped into your think tank right now. Ready?

1. God knows everything (Acts 15:18).
2. God is holy (1 Pet. 1:15–16). He gives you the power to walk in the light.
3. God is love (1 John 4:8). He is vitally interested in your welfare.
4. God is true (Rom. 3:4). He keeps all agreements without grumbling behind your back.
5. God answers to no one (Isa. 40:13–14). What God does for you is not out of a sense of obligation.

6. God is all powerful (Rev. 19:6). You can be secure in His care for you.
7. God is infinite and eternal (Ps. 90:2). He has the perfect viewpoint concerning your suffering.
8. God is unchanging and unchangeable (James 1:17). He is not schizophrenic in His compassionate attitude toward you.
9. God is present everywhere (Ps. 139:7–10). You cannot escape His work in your life.
10. God is righteous and just (Ps. 19:9). He is no respecter of persons.
11. God is the number-one ruler in the universe (Eph. 1:20–23). He has everything under control, including your situation.

Many times we want God to adjust to our way of thinking. When this is our approach, it doesn't take long for us to realize that we are engaged in an exercise of futility. Probably the worst judgment God could bring upon a nation or an individual is to permit us to have our own way on our own terms. If, however, we adjust properly to God's thoughts, we will increase in value to Him as His servants here on earth. We can then step outside our wounds and bring the healing power of the cross of Jesus Christ to others who are hurting. We have categorically adjusted to God's way of thinking.

Bluntly put, God will not adjust to your way of thinking. You may try to manipulate His attention through weeping, pleading, or backsliding. After all is said and done, you will adjust to His thoughts revealed in the Word.

You may blow off steam and act like a fool for a

while, but sooner or later, after total exhaustion, you must reckon with the fact that He will not budge. He is in charge. He is the Creator. You are His creature. Humble Christians have no argument with this reality, because once they understand it they enter into great freedom, living and loving within the boundary lines of their spiritual inheritance.

Here is an additional reality check: Expecting life to be "fair" because you're a good person is like expecting a charging bull to hold off his attack because you're a vegetarian!

PERSONAL REFLECTION OR DISCUSSION

1. What has been your view of God's anger and justice, and has your perspective changed as a result of this chapter?

2. Which of the attributes of God applies to a specific circumstance in your life right now?

3. Think of a time when your emotions ran wild in a difficult situation. How do you view that situation right now? With the benefit of time, what have you learned about yourself and about God?

4. Have you caught a glimpse of God's greatness? Bow your heart before Him and ask for a fresh vision of His greatness and power.

𝐴dam ate the apple and our teeth still ache.

(Hungarian proverb)

CHAPTER

- SIX -

DON'T LOSE YOUR SPIT AND VINEGAR

> Doubts are the ants in the pants that
> keep faith moving.
> — Frederick Beuchner

Spit and vinegar: the resolve to win and succeed in spite of all odds; clenched teeth, gritted in dogged determination; eyes blazing with purpose, eternal purpose; the refusal to compromise godly convictions; despising the easier road, the path of least resistance; that substance which makes one unwilling to retire from the sometimes painful process of growth, even if everything seems to be totally "unfair," the disdain for self-pity and prolonged periods of personal discouragement.

What does it take for you to lose your will to fight? What "unfair" event or series of "unfair" circumstances can force you to consider quitting and throwing in the towel?

It happened to Jeremiah. He lost his spit and vinegar. He was a weeping prophet, aware of the backslidden condition of the nation of Israel, and boldly declaring the truth about the not-so-pleasant consequences looming ahead in their future. Only repentance could stop God's judgment. The more he preached, the more he was rejected. In the 20th chapter of the book written by Jeremiah, he mentions that the chief officer of the temple finally got so enraged by his preaching that he had Jeremiah's hands, feet, and neck firmly secured in a torturous device called stocks and ordered that 40 lashes smite his back without mercy.

All this "unfair" treatment caused Jeremiah to shamelessly complain to the Lord by saying, "You are stronger than I am and You have overpowered me. Everyone makes fun of me; they laugh at me all day long. Lord, I am ridiculed and scorned all the time because I proclaimed your message. Why was I born? Was it only to have trouble and sorrow, to end my life in disgrace?" (Jer. 20:7–18; paraphrased).

I cannot bring myself to criticize Jeremiah as I hear the biting sarcasm in his words. God seemed to be unaware of his plight. Jeremiah had been a faithful servant without due protection and security. You see, I too, have come to the place where I lost my spit and vinegar. Like Jeremiah, I have said, "I will not mention Him or speak any more in His name" (Jer. 20:9; NIV).

I never thought it could happen to me. If you had been on hand to speak with me after my graduation from Bible school, you would have heard nothing but confident statements regarding my assurance of God's presence and power in my life. Full of vitality and enthusiasm, I never would have dreamed that there could come a time in my life when I would want to lie down and die. The mere thought of it was foreign to me.

It was 1982. At 28 years of age, after seven years of full-time Christian service, I entered into a dry period of 10 to 12 months, experiencing no warm, fuzzy feelings. Some people call it a wilderness experience. As a pastor, husband, counselor, and father, I had enjoyed a string of successes; you know, the resume/obituary-type stuff. I had hosted regular radio and television talk shows, planted three healthy churches, enjoyed six years of marriage, three years of being a proud dad, traveled to and preached in over a half-dozen foreign countries, and had successfully ministered to a number of professional athletes.

Suddenly, at a time when everything seemed to be better than ever, a cloud of despair enveloped me as various people began to quietly criticize my leadership and many left my congregation with lame excuses. I was devastated. I didn't know what to do.

I couldn't sense God's presence in my life. My prayer life became virtually non-existent. At best, reading the Bible was tantamount to chewing shredded cardboard. Somehow, I was able to preach when necessary, but even that was a hollow experience. I felt like a fraud, giving advice, teaching, smiling, and joking on the outside, but empty on the inside. There were times when I sat at my desk for hours doing absolutely nothing. As a workaholic, these unproductive hours bombarded me with extreme guilt. There I sat — confused, angry, hurt, and tired — tired of dealing with people, tired of the pain, tired of feeling miserable.

I felt vulnerable. I was struggling. Here I was, smack-dab in the middle of the midnight trial. Thoughts crossed my mind; thoughts I had never before encountered to such a degree; "God is not 'fair.' He disapproves of me and my performance. I must have done something to deserve this. He is out to get me." Theologically, I knew that the content of those thoughts could not be substantiated, but I began to brood over them.

A root of bitterness began to spread out within my heart as circumstances worsened. I intensified my awareness of the "unfairness" of the events surrounding my life and collected data that would justify my increasingly distorted way of thinking. My desire to fight the good fight regardless of the circumstances was slowly but surely being replaced by the desire for a conflict-free environment at any price. I came to the point where I was willing to sell my spit and vinegar for quietness and security, something that I had claimed in my earlier years would never happen. I had maintained that I would never be a "spineless jellyfish."

I cried out to the Lord, "What have I done to deserve all this? I've been faithful to You all these years. I've resisted temptation and to the best of my knowledge, I have an honest, open relationship with the Holy Spirit. I have walked honorably before You."

When my wife asked if there was anything she could do or say that could help, I withdrew into my shell, saying, "Naw, everything's going to work out. I'm okay. Don't worry about me." My communication level with my wife dipped dangerously low as I continued to back away from her offered assistance.

Then, one day, I remembered a real-life story that helped me focus clearly and regain my spit and vinegar. I decided it was time to fight back against the gloominess of my "unfair" situation.

It was a crisp evening in Chicago. As they walked briskly from the restaurant, Jeffrey's wife drew closer to him. She was glad to see him after visiting relatives for a week. Earlier, he had picked her up at the bus station and had surprised her by taking her to a fine restaurant for a leisurely dinner. A few more blocks and they'd be heading for home. As they rounded the final corner they froze as, without warning, two youths jumped out from a darkened alley no more than ten yards in front of them.

With switchblades drawn, the youths advanced. "Hey man, give us all your money or we'll cut you to pieces," they said derisively.

Jeffrey instantly knew what to do. His whole body tensed and then he released a coordinated flurry of hand and feet movement. Within a matter of seconds, both would-be muggers were painfully writhing on the ground. Quickly Jeffrey and Helena ran for their car and off they sped. Squealing tires. Over-the-shoulder looks. Pumping adrenaline.

As I remembered this account, one principle stuck with me: *The sweat of discipline and the hard work of repetition always precede the thrill of spontaneity in any pursuit of life.* Jeffrey, my friend, had no time to think and plan his course of action when the would-be muggers approached. Although he was a martial arts instructor, he had never before been faced with a life-threatening event such as this one. His instant performance of precise body movements, however, had been preceded by years of hard work. He had virtually punished his body into shape by repeatedly practicing, to the point of exhaustion, certain moves until those moves became a part of his automatic reflexes. Under pressure, he didn't panic. Instead he acted instinctively and lived to tell the story, a little older and a little wiser. In a flash, he was able to reap the benefit of years of preparation.

As I sat at my desk that particular afternoon, evaluating my life and recalling this event in Jeffrey's life, the same old thoughts of gloom and doom began to pervade my mind. I got mad and actually said out loud, "Freeman, this is ridiculous! It's time to stop this foolishness and grow up. You've got enough dynamite of the gospel and power of the Word of God to reduce the D.P.S.I. (Demons Per Square Inch) level to zero!"

Instantly, I knew where the poisonous thoughts had come from. They'd been incubated in hell. The Holy Spirit reminded me of the Scripture passage that claims that God's thoughts toward me are thoughts of peace and not evil, to give me an expected end (Jer. 29:11). I also knew that the frenzy of self-pity I had whipped myself into didn't correspond with the benefits of my salvation mentioned in the Bible. Instead of buying into the former thoughts, I determined to retaliate with a vengeance. I guess you could say that I used "mental judo" or "spiritual karate," because without a moment's notice, I whirled into action using the Word of God — a blur of precise mental energy. CRACK! POW! BLAM! ZOW! The demons who were sent on a search-and-destroy mission had to fly for cover as I confronted them with many of the "It is written's" of the Word of God. Using the Scriptures, I confronted the kingdom of darkness with the blood of Jesus, reminding Satan about my standing with Christ as a child of the King of kings and Lord of lords. Along with Jeremiah, I finally said to God, "Your message is like a fire burning deep within me. I try my best to hold it in, but can no longer keep it back."

Exciting? Absolutely! It was fun being a winner — a more-than conqueror! After all, I had already read the back of the Book (the Bible) and had discovered that I had joined the winning team.

As days passed, I began to research diligently what the Bible taught about specific subjects like how to handle fear, anger, and discouragement.

During my life up to this point, I had been gripped by an inordinate need for approval from others. My whole emotional well-being depended upon my perception of the visual and verbal clues that were offered by people around me, communicated in my direction. Personal insecurity and fear had tortured me much of the time, with varying degrees of intensity. In fact, after preaching most messages I would analyze their continuity and try to perceive their effectiveness, usually feeling I could have done much better.

It was therefore no surprise that intensified criticism from some in my congregation hit me in the solar plexus and had such a devastating negative effect on my emotions. At that time I didn't define it as such, but later on I realized I had thought that everyone should appreciate and understand me. It was this distorted way of thinking that caused such suffering within and made me vulnerable to emotional blackmail from others. Guilt trips had forced me to a high level of consistent work performance, trying to win the favor of people in my sphere of influence. My life view was the perfect set-up for me to blame God, saying, "You're not 'fair,' " when circumstances became unpleasant.

I had memorized enough of the Scriptures and knew enough theology to sink a battleship, but now something was different. At this juncture in my life, I felt like Daniel did when he said, "I had no strength left . . . I was helpless" (Dan. 10:7–19). I felt like Jacob

(Gen. 32), limping about because of being touched by God at the point of natural strength. Somehow, Jesus was present, waiting for me to cease trying to work for Him and begin to know Him as my Life, allowing Him to be my all in all.

Little by little, I began to get my spit and vinegar back by filling the rooms of my soul with the Word in the precise categories where I needed the most assistance. I was determined that when (not if) I got into a boxing match with the devil again, he might win the round, but he would never win the decision.

I was intoxicated with my new-found love for Jesus and His Word. Then the tests began to come. Was this a passing fancy or was this to be an established way of being for the rest of my life? Only time would tell.

Personal Reflection or Discussion

1. Have you ever lost your spit and vinegar? If so, try to think of that time.

2. How did that wilderness experience help to make you what you are today?

3. Select four verses of Scripture that can be applied to a current challenge in your life. Write the verses on 3x5 cards and tape them on the four corners of your bathroom mirror. Read them whenever you see them, and ask the Holy Spirit to bring them to your remembrance during each day.

CHAPTER

- SEVEN -

MENTAL JUDO

> Mountaintops inspire leaders, but valleys mature them. — F. Philip Everson

One thing I have realized is that we all struggle where we are planted. Secretaries, scientists, teachers, mothers of three kids, lawyers, athletes, doctors, and preachers all deal with their own stuff. One may look at another person's wrestling match and view it as a trivial pursuit. Yet we all are learning, at our own pace, to strategically fight the right enemy with the right weapons. And most of the time the battleground is our mind.

For 18 years (1975–1993), I pastored three churches in the USA and helped to establish works in Puerto Rico and Dominican Republic. As I look back with 20/20 vision, most of the things I struggled with seem so stupid — now that I have some perspective. Hardly a blip on my radar screen. At the time, however, I was easily caught up with things that hardly seem to matter at this point in my life. I guess they call it the maturation process. Let me give you a sneak peak at some of my struggles and how I fought back. To me, at the time, this was serious stuff.

One morning, I went to visit a pastor in a neighboring town. He and his congregation had purchased a huge school facility, dirt-cheap from the county, for their ministry. It had been only months prior that our congregation had lost out on a similar bid for a school facility in our community. He took me on a grand tour of their marvelous provision.

Internally, I began to think stupid, jealous thoughts motivated by the insecurity of comparing the growth of my church with his. Inwardly I was saying, "It's not 'fair.' He's been pastoring for a much shorter time than I have been pastoring and he didn't even go to Bible school." Outwardly I was exclaiming, "Praise the Lord. This building is tremendous."

Instead of entertaining those negative, critical thoughts, right there I began to employ verses that taught me to rejoice with other members of Christ's body when they rejoiced and get excited when they get blessed (Rom. 12:15; 1 Cor. 12:12–25). As I quietly meditated on these verses while touring the property, I repented to God for my selfish frame of mind, opening my heart to God's love, and closing it to fleshly pettiness. An hour later, I walked to my vehicle with a spring in my step, got in and praised God for the practical lesson I had just encountered. "Mental Judo" was working. I still had my spit and vinegar!

The following Sunday I stood up to preach. I was prepared, but felt dry. In fact, I felt kind of crabby. Maybe it was because my three-year-old son David had drooled toothpaste on my nicest suit earlier that morning as I assisted him with his daily grooming. Or maybe it was because I ran late all morning as the result of a long-winded telephone caller. I can't put my finger on it, but all I know is that I didn't feel too spiritual.

I preached. Oh, yes, I preached. Then I shook
hands with people at the door, played briefly with some
kids, picked up a crumpled bulletin, threw it away,
talked seriously with a needy person, set up a counseling appointment, joked around with some teenag-
ers, gathered the family, and finally got in the car to
drive home. As soon as the car doors shut, I looked at
my wife and asked, "Was the message cohesive? Was
it effective?" Without waiting, I added, "I think the
message bombed this morning." She tried gallantly to
hide the pained here-we-go-again expression on her
face and attempted to encourage me by stating, "Oh,
no, honey, the message was good. Believe me. It was
good."

Upon arrival back home I went to my office and
allowed the Word of God to penetrate my heart (2
Tim. 4:2; 1 Cor. 1:26–31). I fought against the former
way of thinking and literally enjoyed the rest of the
day. As an added bonus, a man called later that afternoon and said, "Joel, I just wanted you to know that
your message this morning has been a blessing to my
heart all day. Thank you for preaching the truth." God
used me by His grace in spite of my immature attitude. What was even more exciting was that I was fighting back, seeing progress and growth right before my
eyes!

In a similar manner, I allowed the Holy Spirit to
expose with clarity other root issues that had been
coddled and embraced for years. For instance, the low
communication level with my wife when I felt discour-
aged. I began to learn that she was my best asset — my
best friend, regardless of the situation. Also, my incli-
nation to avoid conflict when people "unfairly" criti-

cized me for a legitimate decision made by me. I set my will to love them while holding tenaciously to my original choice. Specific study in the Word helped direct my heart into a wholesome state.

I decided that the only way to experience mental and emotional health was to plan purposely to develop God's perspective regarding the details of life. Then and only then could I break the old patterns of automatic reaction and enter into a whole new way of dealing with Satan and his crafty cohorts. Like Jeffrey, in the previous chapter, I was learning how to fight spiritual battles with godly strategy, realizing I had embarked on a journey that included a process I'd never outgrow.

Fight back! That is the theme of adventuresome risk-takers — people who know where they have come from and where they are going. They recognize the realities of the satanic conflict. They understand that Satan thrives upon taking advantage of spiritually exposed people. They have personally experienced the devastating effects of self-pity and have decided to mount a ruthless counterattack with the offensive weaponry of the Word. In the same way that Jeffrey painstakingly rehearsed certain physical procedures in the martial arts, we must also carefully concentrate in the spiritual realm upon the Bible and its holy principles.

This is not accomplished with a defeatist mentality. Resigning ourselves to what some may call a string of bad luck is another way of giving in. Fighting back is vital, but we are permitted to do so with the right weapons, for the right purpose, with the right enemy. We can fight God, the pain, the doctors, or the seeming futility of it all. The greatest enemy, however, is our self. Acceptance of that fact is 90 percent of the fight.

We must diligently study and meditate upon specific Scriptures as the price we pay to have disciplined minds. This means we are to fill our souls with a catalog of major categories and themes.

For instance, if the diabolical one strikes with doubts regarding God's covenant of love and grace toward us, or causes anxiety about God's will in our lives, or raises questions about our eternal salvation, the Holy Spirit immediately reminds us of the needed verses and Satan is promptly dealt a fatal blow by frail sinners saved by grace. Instead of moping about the "unfairness" of life, we decide to channel our energies into productive thinking that honors and glorifies Jesus Christ.

The process of growth is usually longer and harder than previously anticipated. At the risk of sounding simplistic, there is a pertinent scriptural principle to neutralize every mental-attitude sin. With the Holy Spirit's help, fear is removed by the personal reality that "if God is for us, who can be against us?" (Rom. 8:31). Arrogance and self-righteousness are dispelled when we remember that we are not appointed to judge other people (Matt. 7:1–2; Luke 6:37; Rom. 2:1). Vindictiveness and revenge are excluded by taking God at His word when He says, "Vengeance is mine; I will repay" (Rom. 12:19). And we are left with no cause for jealously or envy since our own blessings are sufficient and perfectly timed for our greatest good. For us to maintain our sanity, we must concentrate on what we have, not on what we have not (Matt. 6:25–34). And it is our position to ultimately adjust to God's way of thinking.

The "fairness" issue is a particularly deceptive one

because it is one of the major tactics Satan uses to cause us to lose our spit and vinegar in our most unguarded, vulnerable moments. Biblical themes such as the reality of heaven and hell, God's patience and mercy, or our call to be ambassadors for the King here on earth, are just a few of the many categories that are especially helpful when we are feeling despondent because of our "unfair" circumstances.

Therefore, it is suggested that we employ the discipline and hard work required in studying these and other categories until they become a part of our automatic reflexes. Satan can intimidate sincere Christians who are fuzzy in their thinking with regard to the Word of God. If you've lost your spit and vinegar and seem to be trapped in a pit of despair, there is hope. Don't fear life. Face it with faith and courage.

At the Cross, Jesus Christ won the greatest battle ever fought and has graciously included you and me in that victory. A conqueror has the victory march after he has won the battle, but a more-than-conqueror has the victory celebration before he goes to war. Christ has made us more than conquerors. Which, when translated, means that we never have to entertain fear about the future. Regardless of what happens in the future, we can boldly live in a victorious frame of mind, even when confronted with heartache that causes us to weep, mourn, or grieve like never before.

This reminds me of Michele, a woman in her late fifties. For months I had been counseling with her periodically and at a particularly rough time in her life she said, "I pity women with good marriages." Her quiet statement had taken me by surprise, especially since I knew many of the details of her marriage of 35 years to a domineering man who ruled the house with intimidating words and psychological games. (If there had been physical abuse I would have recommended intervention by the appropriate civil authorities.)

When I asked for clarification, she replied, "My marriage has caused me to get to know the Lord like nothing else could. Without Him, I would have left the marriage a long time ago. As you know, I've had my bags packed on many occasions," she added, with a twinkle in her eyes.

"Several years ago," she continued, "I made the conscious decision to stop taking my martyr pills and to start loving God's Word. Everything in my situation looked terrible, but God's presence became sweeter and sweeter. I know me. A good marriage would have permitted me to get soft and complacent in terms of my relationship with Jesus. As I look back on my life, I wouldn't trade places with anybody!"

Nothing here on this planet earth — no sudden tragedy or long-standing suffering — can rob us of our spit and vinegar. We may lose heart for a season, but joy always is ushered in with a brand-spanking-new phase of maturity in Christ. Our goal is to grow to be like Jesus, never questioning God's plan — always trusting Him spontaneously. Remember, the sweat of discipline and hard work of repetition always precedes the thrill of spontaneity in any pursuit of life.

Did great men like Jonah or Elijah or Job ever lose their spit and vinegar? Let's peek into actual counseling sessions God had with these three men who were hurting so badly at the time that they were each on the verge of suicide.

PERSONAL REFLECTION OR DISCUSSION

1. Think about my definition of *spontaneity*. How has the sweat of discipline and the hard work of repetition paid off in your life?

2. How does the concept of "mental judo" fit into the realm of spontaneity?

3. In what situations have you already used "mental judo"?

CHAPTER

- EIGHT -

THE
ULTIMATE
PSYCHOLOGIST

There are moments when everything
goes well; don't be frightened, it won't last.
— Jules Renard

How would you like to have a counseling session with God? Wouldn't that be wonderful? The next time you feel downright crabby you could call Him. He would appear, and you could lie on your "grouch couch" and gripe about the terrible condition of your life. (Eat your heart out, Sigmund Freud.) Would you care to set up an appointment for next Wednesday afternoon? Before you enthusiastically answer the initial question, let's review some of what we know about God and His justice:

1. God is objective and impartial. He refuses to be manipulated by human reasoning.
2. God sees the motives of the human heart. One may fool some of the people some of the time, but absolutely no one can pull the wool over His eyes at any time.
3. God is holy; therefore, He is more interested in personal holiness than in personal happiness.

4. God emphasizes personal responsibility for behavior. He will not spare us until we see the wickedness of our hearts. Then, He will not stop until we see the power of His grace.

5. God has been known to allow certain people to be stoned, sawn asunder, and tormented to death, without any visible evidence of success in their lives (Heb. 11:36–39).

6. Our ideas are not always in harmony with His.

7. God is compassionate and merciful. He knows how much pain we can take.

Before going too much further, let's see what happens when three people actually had counseling sessions with God in His roving office. Don't forget, these people were hurting emotionally. They were grumpy because they could not control the "unfair" events in their lives. In fact, each one was so distraught that he was seriously toying with that fatal urge — suicide.

The first session was held on a hill overlooking the ancient city of Nineveh, the capitol of the despised Assyrian Empire. Jonah — the proudest, brattiest prophet in the Bible — was in a foul frame of mind. From his vantage point on the hill, he could see well over the walls that ran 80 miles around the extreme outer perimeter of the city. As he continued to survey the scene before him, he observed the five walls and three moats that protected the people of the much smaller inner city that was only three miles long and one and a half miles wide.

The glare of the sun bore down from a cloudless sky. Just hours before, Jonah had perspired his way up the hill, pausing only to glance periodically over his shoulder at Nineveh. It hadn't taken him long to find an inviting rock on which he could rest his weary bones. As his gaze locked into the stone walls of Nineveh, his mind raced. He had a lot to think about.

Some years earlier, as a political representative of Israel, he had negotiated the return of Israel's lost coastal region. He held a deep, patriotic love for his country. His problems, however, had begun when God had commanded him to preach a message of repentance to the arrogant, ruthless Assyrians who were threatening to conquer his beloved nation with their dread military machine. He wasn't about to betray his own people. What if God extended kindness to the enemy because of his message? He had been repulsed at the mere thought and had fled in the opposite direction.

He squinted his eyes as he thought about the events of recent weeks. Who back home would ever believe his story? A storm at sea? Getting thrown overboard just to be promptly swallowed by a huge fish for three days? Being vomited up by the fish and landing on a sandy beach, looking like a bleached alien from another planet? Preaching to his brutal enemies and then watching them repent by the thousands? The worst thing, though, was that God forgave the entire city and showed mercy to this nation that had oppressed His people for years. They deserved total destruction. Was this "fair"?

His thoughts became more and more volatile. "Well, God," he whispered irritably, "I'm waiting. Any moment now, you can wipe 'em off the map." The moments, however, became minutes. The minutes, hours. Perspiration dripped from his forehead. His eyes never wavered from the city, fully expecting fiery judgment to erupt from within its walls.

Finally, out of helpless frustration he bellowed, "God, if You're not going to destroy Nineveh, then I want to die. Go ahead, take my life!"

Jonah's desperate plea was met with silence. Then, the all-knowing, all-powerful God of the universe spoke, asking one penetrating question, pregnant with meaning: "Jonah, what right do you have to be angry?"

It sounded like an elementary question, but it cut down to the root of Jonah's selfishness. God didn't stop there, though. According to Jonah 4, He proceeded to give Jonah a kindergarten object lesson. God caused a large castor oil plant to grow miraculously directly behind him. The resultant shade produced a mood swing in Jonah, from deep depression to exceeding joy. For the remainder of the day, Jonah basked in the cool shadow of the plant, happy as a window salesman after a hurricane.

The next morning, however, a worm attacked the plant and it died just as quickly as it had grown. A scorching east wind blew in with suffocating heat, causing Jonah's mood to swing back to total despair.

After Jonah expressed his second death wish, God confronted the absurdity of Jonah's spiritual apathy toward the welfare of the people of Nineveh. Jonah's primary concern was with his own physical comfort, yet he lacked compassion for the 120,000 little children in Nineveh. Through it all, God exposed Jonah's deep-seated hatred for God's mercies and his inordinate preoccupation with his own ego needs.

God used a plant, a worm, the sun, and a hot summer wind to get His point across. Do you think God used a strange counseling technique? Wait till you see His approach with Elijah!

The second counseling session was in a cave. In

1 Kings 19, Elijah had prayed a 28-second prayer, and fire had come down from heaven. After that tremendous victory, Jezebel had scared the living daylights out of Elijah and he ran almost one hundred miles from Mount Carmel to Beersheba. Needless to say, he was frightened!

Then he ran into the wilderness, plopped himself down under a juniper tree, and wanted to die. To make a long story short, he ultimately ended up in a cave in the mountainside. As he sat there, a strong wind, an earthquake, and a fire occurred in front of him, in that order.

Finally, Elijah heard a still, small voice. No one knows what was said. Then the Lord spoke audibly with this incisive question: "What are you doing here, Elijah?" The prophet didn't respond verbally, but he acted quickly because the next thing we read is that he took off for Damascus to anoint someone as king.

Thus far, God has been light on words but heavy on action. How do you think He handled His next client?

The third session was held in the ashes of a burned-out home. Job had lost hope. He felt forsaken by a God who had used him for a "whipping boy." He thought God had left him to work things out on his own. At one point, he arrogantly said that if he ever found God's throne, his mouth would be filled with arguments. He had lost virtually everything. His three friends were slowly but surely tearing down what little self-esteem he had left.

How would you handle an intense counseling case such as this one? Let's step aside and watch the Great Psychiatrist at work. In Job 38:3, God bluntly commanded, "Stand up now like a man and answer the questions I ask you." In the next two chapters God dazzled Job with fancy footwork. He pulled back the curtains and revealed the incredible power behind nature.

He explained to Job the very foundations of the earth; what kept the sea from covering the entire face of the earth; the beginnings of ice and frost; the exact place where light came forth to shine upon the world; the innumerable stars and galaxies stretching across space; the miraculous beginnings of each morning. The laws of precipitation, evaporation and condensation; the intrigues of the deep sea; the cause of lightning, thunder, and clouds; the intricacies of the animal kingdom; and the perfect harmony of the earth, nature, and the entire universe, from the macro to the micro.

At this point, Job gasped for breath and blurted out, "Behold, I am vile, what shall I answer Thee? I will lay my hand upon my mouth." Instead of getting more depressed, Job began to think, *If God is that powerful — if He is that great — is He not big enough to take care of my problems? I am persuaded that He can take care of me.*

God did not specifically address the "fairness" issue. No camels were raised from the dead. No homes were rebuilt. No children were resurrected. No prayers were dramatically answered. Not one miracle happened — just a childlike trust in God's great authority!

Job stopped justifying himself. Absolutely nothing changed in his environment. The only thing that changed was his attitude toward God. He no longer thought of God as a cruel taskmaster. He saw God as One who was bigger than all his questions about "fairness."

The big question is not, "Why me?" or "Why did that happen?" The real question is, "Why are you and I still alive?" or "Why does God choose to have mercy upon us at all?" Like Job, we are prone to strut into the arena of suffering, mouth first — asking all the wrong questions.

While Jonah never seemed to respond positively, Elijah went from his counseling session with God as a changed man. He no longer was a sniveling crybaby!

God exhibited a rather unique counseling technique with all three men. He was extremely patient, allowing them to function irrationally without instant reprimand. The therapeutic relationships were fostered by His unconditional love for them. He waited for the appropriate moments and then challenged each man with the brutal facts.

The casual observer may decide that God's counseling style was rather abrupt, perhaps unfeeling — even "unfair." However, from our grandstand seats in the 21st century, we can see with 20/20 hindsight that His absolute justice and mercy blended together in perfect counsel — specifically directed to the real needs rather than the perceived needs of each one.

Now, how would you like to have a personal counseling session with God the next time you are adamant about your right to know the answers to all the "why" questions in your life? Would you impudently demand your rights? How about tomorrow? We can schedule an appointment — perhaps at 3:30 in the afternoon?

PERSONAL REFLECTION OR DISCUSSION

1. If you could have anything, what would you ask of God? (See 1 Kings 3:9.)

2. Think for a moment: what trials in your life might God be using to turn your attention to Him?

3. How do you respond when your work goes unrecognized?

4. In light of what you know and have read about the attributes of God, what would His counsel be to you right now?

CHAPTER

- NINE -

HEY, GOD'S GOT RIGHTS, TOO!

How good it is that God above has never gone on strike,

Because He was not treated fair in things He didn't like.

If only once, He'd given up and said, "That's it, I'm through!

"I've had enough of those on earth, so this is what I'll do:

"I'll give my orders to the sun — cut off the heat supply!

And to the moon — no more light, and run the oceans dry.

Then just to make things really tough and put the pressure on,

Turn off the vital oxygen till every breath is gone!"

You know He would be justified if fairness was the game,

For no one has been more abused or met with more disdain

Than God, and yet He carries on, sup-
plying you and me
With all the favors of His grace, and
everything for free.

Men say they want a better deal, and
so on strike they go,
But what a deal we've given God to
whom all things we owe.
We don't care whom we hurt to gain
the things we like,
But what a mess we'd all be in if God
should go on strike.

— Walt Huntley

Have you ever been a red-faced, irate consumer? Have
you ever felt ripped-off by the manufacturer of a product? How about the corduroy pants that shrank two
sizes after the first wash? How about the "lemon" car
that was too young to smoke?

Some people are too embarrassed to complain
about a bad transaction. But most people have no
qualms about making a scene, because they believe in
the old adage, "The squeaky wheel gets the grease."

I'll never forget the man I saw at a car dealership a
number of years ago. He was in the process of raking
the sales manager over the coals for selling him a lemon.
Potential customers were craning their necks to see
what all the fuss was about.

The flustered general manager was present, trying
to bring a sense of order to the whole situation. No
matter how hard he tried, he could not quiet the man
who was boisterously yelling. "Even if I have to stay

overnight, I will stand right here until you give me a new car or give my money back! I'm sick and tired of the lousy hunk of metal you sold me! I've got my rights!"

Some of us can identify with that man, especially those of us who have had similar experiences. We can also understand the rights of the victims of crime, over-taxed citizens, battered wives, unborn children, and prisoners of war. In fact, there is a whole list of special interest groups that have points to make for legitimate cases: women's rights, men's rights, criminal rights, animal rights, patient rights, human rights, constitu-tional rights, states' rights, labor rights, religious rights, civil rights, consumer rights.

Each of these has a degree of legitimacy, but where do we stop? Do we give mothers a right to decide whether they want their unborn children to live? Do we slap a murderer on the wrist because his lawyer successfully argues "temporary insanity"? Do we ex-cuse a high school boy for raping a girl because the judge feels that the boy had been subjected to sexual stimuli in society and was only doing what was natu-ral? Do we make it legal to kill millions of unborn chil-dren while bringing harsh fines and swift imprison-ment for killing bald eagles? Do we adopt the philoso-phy that personal rights and pleasure are more impor-tant than loyalty to marriage vows? Do we continue to allow confessed criminals to escape the consequences of their actions because of foolish technicalities?

At this moment I can hear a sweet, little old lady in the background yelling at the top of her lungs, "Stop asking so many questions. You're depressing me." Whew, I'm glad she interrupted me, because we must pause and give equal time to another set of rights that are rarely considered in the midst of all the hubbub.

What about God's right? Have you ever stopped to think about it? He has allowed himself to be victimized. Over the course of history, man exploited His name for personal gain. He has been hated without cause, slandered without reason, and forgotten without apology. His character has been misrepresented when humans have suffered. His name has been cursed when humans have reaped the results of personal sin. His family has been abused and injured by every kind of irresponsible behavior. At best, His authority has been ignored.

He has been blamed for famine, war, and disease. A tree falls on a car and the insurance company calls it "an act of God." People have killed other people in His name. His wisdom has been mocked by each successive generation. His standards of holiness have always been considered old-fashioned by the sin-soaked society of every era.

Is He big enough to handle all this abuse? Of course He is. He is not insecure. He can take care of himself. But the telling point is that because of His unconditional love, He has chosen to make himself vulnerable. He is wide open to abuse from humans who are especially interested in their own private rights.

In fact, if we want to magnify the "fairness" issue and demand our rights, we'd better be thankful that He doesn't take us upon our requests. Let's face it — we all deserve hell and damnation. There's not an obedient bone or tissue in our bodies. Our hearts are deceitful and desperately wicked. We couldn't objectively determine the proper standard for our rights, even if we tried.

It always amazes me whenever I think of what God could demand of us. He could demand a perfect human response from us at all times without giving us second chances. He has the right to dispense the quick judgment that His justice demands and that we all deserve.

Instead, He has designed a new plan: "Operation Mercy." Even while His rights have been blatantly violated all across this planet, His mercies have not been affected. The rain still falls on the just and the unjust alike. His mercies are new and fresh every morning. One of the mysteries of God is His patience with indifferent humans.

God made us. He also created the world. Therefore, He has the perfect right to be listened to and thanked, even in the midst of pain and suffering. He deserves the right to be loved and respected above any relationship, material possession, or pursuit of life.

It warms and encourages my heart every time I think of Jan. Back in 1986 I attended her funeral. At the age of 29 she graduated into the glorious presence of Jesus after suffering most of her life from a serious heart and lung condition.

Her primary motivation in life was to honor God's right to be trusted. Even in the midst of her continual pain and uncertainty, she praised His name. Her entire schedule was filled with an all-consuming drive to minister to others beyond the limits of her own four walls. With her husband, Randy, she did so through prayer, telephone calls, and notes of love.

Oh, sure, she had her sometimes-extended periods of questions, negativity, and doubts, but she always came through with a greater determination to amplify God's rights above her own. Jan's life has left a legacy of love and a heritage of hope to the many people who were the recipients of her thoughtfulness.

We, like Jan, must carefully protect His right to be worshipped and served above all others regardless of our circumstances. Great blessings are heaped upon those who honor His right to be trusted, even in the midst of heartrending trials of faith.

If God's rights were honored and guarded, almost every other human right that demands instant attention would be non-existent. "Fairness" would no longer be the issue that energizes so many causes. Wounded individuals would submit to God's Word instead of wallowing in self-pity.

I'm not quick to judge, however, because I have been exactly where they are — filled with self-pity. Each time, I am reminded of my need to pray for others and keep my own fuss budget balanced.

PERSONAL REFLECTION OR DISCUSSION

1. In the past year, in what ways have you honored God's rights?

2. How can you sharpen your spiritual focus on Him who is invisible?

3. Meditate for a few minutes on the mystery of God's patience toward you. Think of a recent time when you behaved like an impudent brat. Thank Him for His long-suffering with you.

4. How will you respond to Him the next time He allows a trial to come your way?

CHAPTER

- TEN -

How to Balance Your Fuss Budget

> God whispers in our pleasures but
> shouts in our pains. Pain is His megaphone
> to rouse a dulled world.　　— C.S. Lewis

Wouldn't it be fun to spend money without ever worrying about the state of your bank account? Ah, yes, it would make one feel footloose and fancy-free. Not a care in the world. Just spend, spend, spend!

I recently grinned mischievously when I saw a person wearing a button that read: WHEN THE GOING GETS TOUGH, THE TOUGH GO SHOPPING. I couldn't help it. It struck me funny and I actually giggled out loud as we walked past, much to the embarrassment of my wife. Later on, after I regained my composure, I went into a deep thought about the spiritual implications of that slogan.

When the going gets tough, many people react violently and expend great amounts of mental and emotional energy with zero productivity as the net result. Their useless thinking leads to useless activity.

For instance, notice how far Elijah ran in 1 Kings 19, after his tremendous victory on the top of Mount Carmel. A few hours after the Mount Carmel victory, Jezebel told him she was going to kill him, and his mind became so filled with fear that he literally ran almost one hundred miles to escape her wrath.

Elijah's futile expenditure of energy was almost as crazy as the activity of Adam and Eve in the Garden of Eden (Gen. 3). After they ate of the forbidden fruit, they began the foolish action of sewing fig leaves together to cover their nakedness. I have never seen a fig leaf, but I am told that, when fully grown, they are about the size of a small dinner plate. And a fig leaf, when picked off the tree, shrinks to the size of a teacup within 24 hours. Does useless thinking lead to needless activity? Of course it does!

That's why it is important to budget the account of our minds with detailed instructions from the Word. If we don't, we will come up short when life presents us with a bill that demands immediate response.

I can speak with a measure of authority on this subject because I have allowed overspending in my fuss budget more than once in my life. Many times I have allowed my emotions to become the boss of my attitude, thereby permitting myself the right to fuss excessively when I felt that life had treated me "unfairly."

As a youngster, if a playmate called me a "dummy," I would run away mad. If my older brother Steve were granted a special privilege, I'd blubber about the "unfairness" of the decision. If my younger sister Beth got away with something that I didn't get away with at her age, I'd grumble. I expended much of my mental and emotional resources focusing on the "fairness" of my circumstances at school, at home, and on the playground. Little did I realize that progressively the fuss part of my emotional budget was developing uncontrollable spending habits.

Events accumulated, and at the age of 17 I found myself arrogantly standing in the doorway of my bedroom with hands stuffed deeply in my pockets, telling my father that I hated him and everything he stood for. As circumstances became more intolerable, I decided to leave my home in Alberta, Canada, to hitchhike aimlessly around North America. On a cold wintry morning, I did just that. I stuck out my thumb with $24 in my pocket and was gone from the restrictions. Free at last! Or so I thought. If I were to give snapshots of my adventures on the road, they would include:

1. Trying to hitch a ride, 20 miles from civilization, in the middle of the Canadian Rocky Mountains with a road-closing snowstorm brewing. (Anxious.)
2. Valiantly selling magazines in Vancouver, British Columbia, trying to make a buck. (Disillusioned.)
3. Spending almost three weeks in a juvenile prison in Portland, Oregon. (Terrified.)
4. Trying to hitch a ride for 15 hours — stuck in Lodi, California. (Frustrated.)
5. Shoveling snow from many doorsteps in Seattle, Washington. ($58 richer.)
6. Panhandling and shoplifting in Victoria, British Columbia. (Excited.)
7. Conning a minister in Banff, Alberta. ($30 richer.)

8. Sleeping beside the road in Weed, California. (Lonely.)

9. Sitting in an evening church service as a long-haired hippie, after taking drugs and drinking beer at an afternoon party in Boothbay Harbor, Maine. (Amused.)

10. Cruising through the Sierra Nevada Mountains of California in a Kharmann-Ghia at 90 mph while the owner of the car slept. (Exhilarated.)

11. Working as a baker's helper in a fancy Portland, Maine, restaurant. (Bored.)

12. Sleeping under the stars in a town park somewhere in a western province of Canada, with hippie-hating cowboys boisterously drinking beer and carousing not more than 200 feet away. (Scared.)

My personal public-relations program told everyone that I was carefree, but, on the inside, I was empty with no resources left to draw from. I was burdened down with the debt of guilt. I had built my apparent happiness upon the despair of others, namely my parents. Without realizing it, I had manipulated myself into carrying the deep root of crybabyitis.

I knew something had to change. And something did change after my conversion to Jesus Christ on September 10, 1972, and entrance into Bible school on the very next day. I began to learn some life-changing principles that assisted me in balancing my fuss budget.

One such principle that especially helped curb the massive spending program of my emotions was The Doctrine of All or Nothing:

ALL

"For all things are for your sake" (2 Cor. 4:15).

"And all things are of God" (2 Cor. 5:18).

"And we know all things work together for good" (Rom. 8:28).

"For of Him, and through Him, and to Him are all things" (Rom. 11:36).

"And every man that striveth for the mastery is temperate in all things" (1 Cor. 9:25).

"Charity . . . beareth all things, believeth all things, hopeth all things, endureth all things" (1 Cor. 13:7).

"The God of all comfort; who comforteth us in all our tribulations . . ." (2 Cor. 1:3–4).

". . . that ye, always having all sufficiently in all things . . ." (2 Cor. 9:8).

"Him who worketh all things after the counsel of His own will . . ." (Eph. 1:11).

"Do all things without murmurings and disputings" (Phil. 2:14).

"I count all things but loss" (Phil. 3:8).

"Casting all your care upon Him; for He careth for you" (1 Pet. 5:7).

". . . the God of all grace . . ." (1 Pet. 5:10).

"And God shall wipe away all your tears" (Rev. 21:4).

NOTHING

"Let nothing be done through strife or vainglory" (Phil. 2:3).

"For we brought nothing into this world, and it is certain we can carry nothing out" (1 Tim. 6:7).

"But let patience have her perfect work, that ye may be perfect [mature] and entire, wanting nothing" (James 1:4).

"For without Me you can do nothing" (John 15:5).

". . . and have not charity, I am nothing" (1 Cor. 13:2).

". . . with God nothing shall be impossible" (Luke 1:37).

". . . the flesh profiteth nothing . . ." (John 6:63).

"Great peace have they which love Thy law [Word]: and nothing shall offend them" (Ps. 119:165).

As you have already noticed, each verse has either the word "all" or "nothing." The remarkable conclusion is that when the word "all" is used, it means all — not 99.9 percent. When the term "nothing" appears, it means just that, absolutely nothing. There's no room for debate, rationalization, or calculated indifference.

The uniqueness and extenuating circumstances surrounding our lots in life may cause us to view these verses with a jaundiced eye. We, however, are invited to come to terms with life's raw deals by submitting willingly to God's plan in God's way, in God's timing — hence The Doctrine of All or Nothing.

I discovered The Doctrine of All or Nothing one day quite by accident after being deeply offended by the way a Bible school classmate had "unfairly" treated me. We had traded some heated words and I retreated to my bedroom, an emotional mess. I was almost ready to settle down, nurse my grudge, and plot revenge, when something inside motivated me to pick up my Bible. I don't do this often, nor do I highly recommend it, but I shut my eyes, twirled the Bible around, opened it, and placed my index finger on a page, hoping it didn't say, ". . . and Judas . . . went and hanged himself."

Much to my great surprise, my finger had pointed to the Psalm 119:165 text quoted above. I was flabbergasted! I stared at the word "nothing" and immediately began to rationalize. I tried valiantly to make it mean something else, but I couldn't. I wanted to talk myself into having a pity party, but that verse kept bombarding my heart with specific truth. I couldn't fight it and maintain an honest relationship with the Holy Spirit at the same time. Before long, I embarked on an intensive study, formulating a personal conviction regarding The Doctrine of All or Nothing. This conviction enabled me not only to repent for the sourpuss attitude I had harbored toward my colleague, but also to ask for and receive forgiveness for the wrongs I had committed against my parents during the rebellion of my youth.

As a result, I was able to balance my fuss budget with the inescapable light from the Word of God. When my camouflaged condition of crybabyitis started acting up because of some pain in the neck harassing me, I learned to rest upon the fact that all things were for my sake.

Personal trauma offers us the opportunity to experience a precious treasure — an understanding heart, a tender heart, a heart filled with mercy.

Personal Reflection or Discussion

1. How are you balancing your fuss budget in light of God's Word?

2. How do you respond when God says no?

3. What are you taking for granted, for which you could be expressing gratitude?

4. Who is there in your past that you need to forgive? What does it take to bring closure to some painful memories?

There's a wideness in God's mercy,

Like the wideness of the sea;

There's a kindness in his justice,

Which is more than liberty.

(Frederick William Faber,
1814–1917)

CHAPTER

- ELEVEN -

MERCY REWROTE A LIFE

> We all agree that forgiveness is a beau-
> tiful idea until we have to practice it.
> – C. S. Lewis

It was Sunday. I had just finished preaching and the service had ended. While talking with various people, I caught sight of a familiar, rather successful business-man in his late twenties (I'll call him Ron). He was standing alone, glancing periodically in my direction. His countenance revealed much about his emotional state. It was the way he stood with shoulders stooped slightly, hands in pockets, leaning against the wall. The way he nervously looked at me with needy, sad eyes — pleading for some kind of help. His dark, disheveled hair and somewhat rumpled casual clothes. The entire scene compelled me to walk over to him. Within seconds, my arm was around Ron's shoulders and without a word we walked to an area where we could talk privately. For a moment he stood silently, biting his lower lip, looking over my shoulder as if feeling guilty for taking me from my conversation with others.

"Is everything all right?" I queried, breaking the silence.

"No," he responded, shifting his weight from one foot to the other. "I don't know what to do. I'm at wit's end." In the quietness, I couldn't help but notice how rapidly tears filled his eyes and then spilled onto his cheeks. *The tears are so close to the surface*, I thought, *he must be experiencing intense pain.* I interrupted my observations with a silent prayer: Lord, grant me wisdom. Make me an instrument of Your healing love and care.

By now Ron's weeping was profuse. He tried to control himself without success.

The last time I had seen him, he was confident, well groomed, and had carried himself in a professional, yet personable manner. What a stark contrast! Standing before me was a vulnerable, despondent man overwhelmed with hopelessness.

I put my arm around his shoulders again. After a few minutes, he heaved a big sigh and began his story.

"Yesterday I discovered that my wife has been having an affair with one of my best friends," he blurted. "I don't know what to do. When I confronted her, she packed her things and moved in with him. It was a big scene. Last night I scared the hell out of myself. I almost blew my brains out with a pistol."

He paused, as if allowing the shock value to penetrate. "For months I knew something was wrong, you know — late nights, stupid excuses, and odd behavior — but I just kept denying it. I kept pushing everything out of my mind. Well, yesterday morning she had left for part of the day and I was cleaning out the attic. In an old suitcase I accidentally stumbled upon a cache of love notes that must go back six or seven months. I began reading the notes he had written to her and I couldn't believe the stuff he wrote! He was tearing me down left and right. And I thought he was my friend. I can't believe it."

It was a paradox. His eyes were red and swollen. His cheeks were partially moist with some powdery patches of dried tears. Yet at the same time, he began unloading the sordid details found in the notes in an increasingly calm, forced manner.

Finally his speech relaxed and he reflected, "You know, Joel, I don't know if this makes any sense to you, but I feel like a total fool. Do you remember the popular song by the Bee Gees about the man who started a joke and got the whole world laughing, but then discovered that the joke was on him?"

"Yes," I replied.

"Well, that's me. I'm the one everybody's laughing at. I'm the fool. I feel like the wind has been knocked out of me. I'm going crazy with anger, jealousy, and wanting to get revenge. I want to hurt him real bad." His voice carried a subdued tone. "Please help me. I'm trapped. I don't want to live and yet I don't want to die."

After listening intently, I knew that he would need long-term support to help him through the challenges of denial, wounded pride, retaliation, self-righteousness, and acceptance. He was like a drowning man, thrashing wildly about, searching for a solution.

I shared some words of encouragement and prayed with him. He gladly accepted my offer to visit together on a weekly basis. During the initial sessions, Ron poured out his heart, expressing a mixture of hatred, guilt, fear, and embarrassment. Many times I looked into his eyes with nothing to offer but my friendship and concern. At those moments, it seemed as though a million questions bombarded my mind. What could I possibly say that would remotely touch his intense encounter with trauma? Why did I feel so awkward and inadequate in his tearful presence? How could I offer advice that didn't sound like a pat answer or a religious cliché? How could I understand the deep pain in his soul and yet challenge him to develop a stable mental attitude?

Over a period of weeks, Ron said he could not sleep many nights and that Psalm 25 was a chapter he would read repeatedly. As I looked at the verses, I could clearly see the pain in his soul. These verses especially seemed to reveal his struggle:

> My eyes are ever on the Lord, for he will release my feet from the snare. Turn unto me and be gracious to me, for I am lonely and afflicted. The troubles of my heart have multiplied, free me from my anguish. Look upon my affliction and my distress and take away all my sins (Ps. 25:15–18; NIV).

After a few more sessions, he seemed to slowly accept personal responsibility for actions which contributed to the breakdown of his marriage. Finally, I gave him an assignment between counseling sessions. Ron's homework was to do a thorough study on the subject of mercy and report back.

The following week, he excitedly entered my office with an overwhelming number of conclusions about the prescribed subject. His countenance was different. His voice carried the ring of renewed vitality. Naturally, I was skeptical about the longevity of such dramatic change. But as I listened to the details of his discovery, I could not help but be drawn by the convincing manner in which he presented the information. The following is a condensed version of his findings:

1. Except for the Lord's mercies, every human being in the world would be consumed (even the innocent victim of an affair) (Lam. 3:22).
2. God concluded that every human was a dirty, rotten sinner, so that He could have mercy upon everybody (Rom. 11:32).
3. God is a multi-billionaire when it comes to mercy (Eph. 2:4).
4. Christians can't even present their bodies as living sacrifices unless they first have received God's mercy (Rom. 12:1).
5. Mercy actually jumps up and down for joy because of the great triumph over judgment (James 2:13).
6. Mercy gives a tailor-made provision for every human pressure, enabling people to see the glory of Jesus Christ instead of fainting (2 Cor. 4:1).
7. All the requirements of truth are satisfied by mercy (Ps. 85:10).
8. The only way Christians can give mercy is if it is first received on a personal basis (Matt. 5:7).
9. Present-day Christians are given the same sure mercies that King David received throughout his lifetime (Acts 13:34).
10. If God could be merciful with the clever manipulator Jacob, there's hope for others (Gen. 32:10).

11. God's mercy endures forever (Ps. 136:1).
12. Recognition of personal sin is the prerequisite to receiving mercy (Matt. 9:13).
13. Mercy is one of the basic principles that modern-day Pharisees forget (Matt. 23:23).

Ron concluded his enlightening discourse by showing how, in the not-so-distant past; he had been embittered by his wife's extra-marital affair. He had been paralyzed by the "unfairness" of the entire situation. Now he realized that, despite the hurt he felt from his wife's wicked sin of adultery, God had worked the situation for his good. It was the first time in his life that he had been driven to his knees in passionate prayer, to recognize his human goodness as unacceptable in God's sight and plead for His mercy! We wept together in my office, praising God for His mercy.

As with Job, nothing had changed outwardly. Ron's wife was still gone, threatening divorce. His home was still lonely. His wife's side of the bed was still cold at night. His wife's lover was still arrogantly flaunting a repulsive lifestyle. But something had changed — Ron's attitude.

He stopped justifying himself. He quit blaming himself and others. He refrained from gazing at his own navel in self-pity, depression, and self-analysis. Instead, he decided to fight back with objective truth from the Word of God. He acknowledged his drastic need for mercy and focused the attention of his heart upon the King of kings and Lord of lords, Jesus Christ. I continued to counsel Ron for a short time after that. I saw him grow by leaps and bounds.

Much later, I took advantage of an opportunity to

see how Ron was progressing. It saddened me to hear of his wife's ultimate decision to reject his attempts at reconciliation and divorce him. However, I was heartened by his settled conviction about the matter. In spite of all the hurtful events that had transpired up to that moment, he was joyful about the new-found maturity he was experiencing.

I have concluded that the secret of Ron's physical, mental, emotional, and spiritual health was his decision to continue in the spirit of mercy. When he awakened every morning, he thanked God for the mercy, which allowed him to be alive for another day. When he ate his breakfast, he acknowledged that because of God's mercy he could chew and digest his food.

His ability to function well on the job was appreciated because of mercy. He was grateful for every small detail in life. The disciplined attitude of gratitude caused him to steer away from the debilitating effects of self-pity and propelled him into an exciting adventure, giving mercy as freely as it was received. Mercy was like a telescope that brought the heavenly perspective into sharp focus.

PERSONAL REFLECTION OR DISCUSSION

1. Is God rewriting your life as He did for Ron?

2. How have God's mercies affected you during this past year?

3. Someone has said that God's mercy withholds what we deserve and His grace gives us what we do not deserve. Think about that which you rightfully deserve in the eyes of a Holy God and that which you do not deserve, but which God in His love bestows upon you. Rejoice today in His mercy and grace.

CHAPTER

- TWELVE -

WOW!
IT'S REAL!

Happiness and depression never mix.
Joy and sorrow mix all the time.

— Anonymous

Q. What is 1,500 miles square, is enclosed by a sheer wall 216 feet thick, with 12 gates made of pearl (from rather large oysters, I presume), and 12 foundations made of precious stones like beryl and amethyst, has streets constructed of pure, transparent gold (no prospecting allowed), has custom-built mansions of indescribable beauty, has no ambulance sirens, no pain, no tears, no death, no darkness; has a crystal clear river with fruitful trees on either bank, has an innumerable company of angels flying about, has a sea of glass (with fish in it, I hope), has people from earth who have graduated to it, and above all, has the throne of God with a green rainbow overhead?

A. Heaven

Can you sense the excitement? This is an attempt to describe the place that is promised to those who have made the choice to follow Jesus. This is the location where crowns and rewards will be given to those who have received Jesus as personal Savior and who have faithfully performed the details of the kingdom of God with dignity. This is the city where all secrets will be revealed and where all wrongs will be righted. This is the place where all "why?" questions will be answered. This is our destiny!

Upon our arrival in that beautiful city we'll fall to our faces at the feet of Jesus. We'll look up, seeing Him in all His glory and splendor — face to face with the One who knows everything about us and still loves us. Then we'll see the nail prints in His hands and feet and the mark of the spear point in His side (the only things in heaven that are made by humans). We'll be overwhelmed by His personal attention.

As eternity unfolds, we will also want to interview all the saints of old. We will ask Elijah to tell the inside story about his dramatic departure from earth to heaven in a fiery chariot. We will ask Methuselah how many push-ups he could do at 968 years of age. We will want to participate in Peter's excitement as he relates his secret for successful water walking. Then, we will ask to hear Rahab's story of how her house stood while the walls of Jericho collapsed. As each one shares his or her personal adventure, something will be unique about each one. None of them will be griping about the "unfairness" of God.

In reality, Job won't be grumbling about his earthly trials. Moses won't be grouching about his wilderness journey. John the Baptist won't be complaining about the loss of his head. David won't be grumping about his troubles with Saul. Each one will magnify the perfect justice and mercy of God. They will refer to every human event from an eternal perspective.

Won't it be refreshing? Just imagine: Every com-

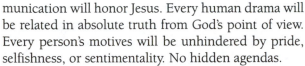

munication will honor Jesus. Every human drama will be related in absolute truth from God's point of view. Every person's motives will be unhindered by pride, selfishness, or sentimentality. No hidden agendas.

After speaking with a host of saints and angels, we will probably want to make our way to a little-known mansion. (Before continuing, allow me to put my tongue in my cheek.) Equipped with thousands of video consoles, it is called "Comedy Palace." This palace is there for the personal enjoyment of each Christian.

We will be able to push a button and instantly re-call selected earthly moments when we were depressed, anxious, or angry. From our heavenly vantage point we will be able to see the real reasons behind our reactions. We'll chuckle reverently as we replay those instances when circumstances seemed dark and gloomy and it felt like God was on vacation. We'll giggle when we see how brattishly we behaved when we thought God was treating us "unfairly," thinking that maybe we were the brunt of some celestial practical joke.

We will be able to laugh at human responses to life's situations because we will possess the perfect ability to know as God knows. We'll see how valuable it would have been to live with a constant hope, undiminished by problems. While basking in heaven's glory, we will see that all our emotional and physical turmoil was nothing when compared to the splendor of eternity.

As I put my tongue back in place, let's meditate on the reality of that beautiful city. When things get tough here on earth, let's allow His perspective to become ours. When tragedy strikes, we can permit the tears to flow while yielding to the sweetness of His presence. When the intensity of the battle becomes much more than we originally bargained for, let's not become grim; instead, let's enjoy a practical sense of humor and keep on keeping on, never losing our fervent passion for His Word.

When all is said and done, God owns everything. He owns our children, our bodies, our finances, and our spouses. He holds our past, present, and future in the palm of His hand. We are stewards, but not owners. He gives. He takes away. Blessed be the name of our Lord. Naked we enter into this world and naked we go from it.

What helps us experience heaven while on earth? What assists us in keeping eternal value in clear view? What keeps us joyfully advancing when every bone and tissue in our body is yelling, "Quit! Throw in the towel"? What shows us the clear lines separating stewardship and ownership? What reveals the immortal justice of God?

The cross of Jesus Christ....

PERSONAL REFLECTION OR DISCUSSION

1. If you were provided the opportunity to visit "Comedy Palace," what would be three "unfair" events you would observe on the video console? How do you think you would react?

2. In view of Nehemiah 8:10, in what ways does the joy of the Lord strengthen you?

3. Name three things about heaven that make your present suffering worthwhile.

CHAPTER

- THIRTEEN -   *SCANDALIZED!*

> I know that God won't give me any-
> thing I can't handle. I just wish He wouldn't
> trust me so much.   – Mother Teresa

Pause and think, just for a moment, about the spot-
less Lamb, Jesus Christ. On the Cross, He accomplished
what no self-help program could do. With excruciating pain, He took upon His precious body the sins of
the entire world — past, present, future. He became
our sin, reeking with the wicked, vile stench of adultery, homosexuality, thievery, pride, bitterness, lying,
and rebellion. He identified with us to such a degree
that His Father could not look upon Him as He paid
the penalty for our sins.

He glared at death, as if to say, "Where is your sting?
Where is your holding power?"

He stared at every foul demon in hell, as if to say,
"Where is your plan? Where is your strength?"

He scrutinized Satan as if to say, "Where is your
fulfillment? Where is your satisfaction?"

He gazed at every human being who ever lived as
if to say, "I love you this much. Will you receive My
death as the payment for your sins?"

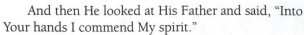

And then He looked at His Father and said, "Into Your hands I commend My spirit."

He finished His work. He accomplished His mission. He died.

With the Cross in clear view, permit me to ask some probing questions:

What is your primary support system in life? Is it your health? Your job? Your family? Your wealth?

To what do you turn in the midst of a crisis? Do you panic? Do you eat a lot? Do you sleep a lot? Do you work a lot?

How do you react when treated "unfairly"? Do you want revenge? Do you rant and rave behind closed doors? Do you harbor bitterness? Do you ache quietly?

While these questions are difficult to answer, at times we become sickened by the conditions of our hearts. At every funeral we become painfully aware of our mortality. We clearly see how fragile we are. We see how quickly tragedy can strike. (At one moment they were in the car, laughing and joking. A split second later, they were dead.) It's easy to become cynical. It's easy to develop an existential posture — life without meaning.

In our search for answers, we turn to the Bible, hoping to find meaning in the midst of a suffering world. Our brows become furrowed as we come across some of the following hard sayings from the lips of Jesus, wondering why He seems to be making life more complicated than it already is:

> Do not suppose that I have come to bring peace to the earth. I did not come to bring peace, but a sword. For I have come to turn a man against his father, a daughter

against her mother, a daughter-in-law against her mother-in-law (Matt. 10:34–35; NIV).

Follow me, and let the dead bury their own dead (Matt. 8:22; NIV).

If anyone would come after me, he must deny himself and take up his cross and follow me (Matt. 16:24; NIV).

Jesus . . . said, "Go, sell everything you have and give to the poor, and you will have treasure in heaven. Then come, and follow me." At this the man's face fell (Mark 10: 21–22; NIV).

Unless a kernel of wheat falls to the ground and dies, It remains only a single seed (John 12:24; NIV).

As we read these harsh statements from Jesus, we may struggle with various rationalizations: We may want to believe that He meant something entirely different for the people who were actually in His presence. Maybe Jesus didn't really mean to make such stringent demands upon weak, frail human beings. Or possibly, He was merely reacting to the unique social pressures of that particular time in human history that are unrelated to the challenges of contemporary Christianity.

Whatever our automatic responses may be, the truth of the matter is that Jesus' all-or-nothing message is just as vital today as it was when He walked the earth. He came to die so that we might live.

Some 2,000 years ago, Jesus was confronted by hearts that were spiritually cold and indifferent. It

doesn't take very long for the careful student of the
Scriptures to realize that gentle Jesus went out of His
way to offend various people. At one point, the disciples cautioned Jesus by telling Him that the Pharisees were offended by His actions and words (Matt.
15:12). On another occasion, the Pharisees were motivated by hard-core bitterness as they tried to belittle
Him with the scathing words, "Is not this the carpenter, the son of Mary?" (Mark 6:3). Can you hear the
disdain in their voices?

Jesus healed on the Sabbath and allowed His disciples to pluck corn on the Sabbath. All of this was
calculated to produce a response that revealed the true
hearts of casual observers. He offended even His disciples on a number of occasions (Mark 14:27–29).

In order for us to understand this properly, we must
find the meaning of the word "offend" in the Greek
language. The original rendering is *skandalizo*[1] from
which we get the English term "to scandalize." The word
literally means to shock a person by outrageous means,
which in turn arouses human prejudice.

In the New Testament, Jesus discerned many "sacred cows" among the people of His day. He then went
about diligently smashing each "sacred cow." Of course,
this action was not enthusiastically received. Hatred
for Him grew with each passing day. At the appointed
time, He set His face toward Jerusalem to die.

Why did the multitudes turn against this One who
cared enough to speak the truth? The answer is simple.
He refused to co-exist with sentimental relationships.
He brought the authenticity of the Cross into every
transaction.

It is interesting to note that upon His death His

disciples were deeply offended, or shall we say, scandalized by Him. His crucifixion caused fear, anger, and disillusionment to penetrate the heart of each disciple. Without the Cross, they probably would have gone through life struggling with superficiality and periodic backsliding. But, thanks be to God, they were confronted with and outraged by the fact that Jesus the Messiah, their Messiah, was crucified in weakness! Before Calvary, they had a passive understanding of who Jesus really was, but after the Resurrection and Pentecost, their convictions about Jesus caused them to be fearless soldiers of the Cross. Every disciple was tortured and flogged. According to tradition, eleven of the disciples finally faced a cruel martyr's death without wavering:

1. Peter — crucified with head downwards.
2. James, son of Zebedee — the sword.
3. John — natural death (after surviving a cauldron of boiling oil).
4. Andrew — crucified slowly (bound by cords).
5. James, son of Alphaeus — crucified.
6. Thomas — spear thrust.
7. Simon — crucified.
8. Bartholomew — crucified.
9. Thaddaeus — killed by arrows.
10. Matthew — the sword.
11. James, brother of Jesus — stoned.
12. Philip — crucified.[2]

Something great had happened! The disciples were changed. Calvary's weakness had to precede their infilling of power and direction by the Holy Spirit at Pentecost. They now had power over death.

The Messiah had come as God's trump card. The innocent suffered for the guilty. This Promised One had introduced a startling idea. Peter Kreeft, professor of philosophy and wordsmith, states this reality in a most engaging manner.

> The most direct and simple answer to the problem of death is resurrection — an answer so simple it's hilariously funny. The resurrection is the biggest joke in history, a joke on all the philosophers who seek to explain death, and on all the mystics who seek to rise above it in spirit. Jesus rose above it in the body! How utterly crass, crude, and direct! The divine style is as subtle as the big bang. Just the thing a child would think of. God never grows up.[3]

The great Christian writer A.W. Tozer once commented that God cannot use a person until he or she has been hurt deeply (and, therefore, those of us who have been hurt deeply can take comfort). As in Bible times, pain seems to be one of the only messages we can clearly understand. God uses it to get our attention.

Emotional pain caused by "unfair" circumstances is hard to bear. When we get hurt, we become irrational and unreasonable. God uses physical and emotional suffering, however, to create an environment whereby we ultimately are forced to confront our inability to continue in human strength.

Usually God uses people as instruments in this process, so we also struggle with hatred and revenge. We focus on people (rather than God's plan), which scandalizes us and arouses our prejudices. By focusing on the "fairness" of our circumstances, we lose the whole purpose of the God-ordained trial and slowly grind ourselves into the ground with a root of bitterness.

God uses people, places, and things to cause us to face the wickedness of our hearts. It is then that we fall down at the front of the Cross to humbly receive His tailor-made provision of forgiveness and mercy for our specific need. He takes our acknowledged sin, casts it in the deepest sea, and then fills us with resurrection power to meet the next challenge.

It is rare in this modern age to find people who have gone through devastating circumstances and have entered into the realm of spiritual maturity with "treasures hidden in darkness and riches stored in secret places" (Isa. 45:3). It is unusual to find those who have crashed through the maturity barriers of moods, mental blocks, and prejudices that have challenged them in the midst of personal trauma.

The popularization of an incomplete gospel message has inoculated the masses with a mere caricature of Jesus, causing many to know Him as Savior, but not as Lord. The offense of the Cross is considered vulgar, while the modern gospel of convenience is popularized.

In the thick of severe testings, it is easy to withdraw our absolute trust in His sovereignty. That is why we must not only comprehend the meaning of the Cross, but we must also take up our cross (our place of death — our electric chair, if you will) daily and apply the principles of death, burial, and resurrection in every detail of our lives.

With abundant clarity we see that there are no caste systems, no race distinctions, no human opinions, and no all-consuming "fairness" questions. At the foot of the Cross, we learn to operate in faith without emotional support. We realize that we are not our own; we have been purchased by a great price — the precious blood of Jesus (1 Cor. 6:20).

This allows us to conclude that God uses people, places, and things as tools to bring us to our wits' ends. Money will not be needed in heaven. But on earth, it is a tool used to teach us the adventures of stewardship. Marriage as we currently know it will not be realized in heaven. But on earth it is a sacred means by which God can teach us the art of forgiveness and unconditional love. Diseased and paralyzed bodies will not be present in eternity. But in this world, they can provide great opportunities for people to experience patience, quietness, and confidence. Unjust criticism will not be heard in paradise. But here on this planet we learn to face it with honesty, mercy, and a sense of humor.

Instead of allowing human events to stop us, we progress in a perpetual forward motion, permitting the death of the Cross to scandalize us by striking at the root of personal selfishness. In turn, we step outside of our puny worlds and minister the resurrection love of Jesus Christ to those who are imprisoned by self-pity because of "unfair" circumstances.

Earl was this type of guy. I heard him preach to a bunch of inmates in the state penitentiary. What a powerful message he gave as he told his life's story!

Right from the start, his life was doomed. "I was

born in the ghetto of New York City. My mama was a whore. I never knew my daddy. From early on, I learned to steal for survival. By the age of nine, I had joined a gang, was hooked on drugs, and had taken part in five murders. The law was constantly on my tail."

As I listened to this short, compact man of swarthy complexion, I was deeply touched by his intensity. He went on to relate a horror story filled with true but almost unbelievable events. I wondered how anyone could survive. Yet, his voice became tender as he shared how Christ had changed his life and had given him a new purpose for living. It was as if his words were transporting everyone's imagination out of that cold, sterile meeting room and into the presence of the living God. There was hardly a dry eye in the place. Even the guards were visibly moved by the drama.

Earl had every legitimate reason under the sun to give up and be a failure. But instead he was allowing the Cross to work the love of Christ into his life. He still had a long way to go, but out of his pain had come a potent ministry of genuine hope to many who were hurting.

In summary, there is no way to avoid emotional wounds. Pain is a realistic part of being alive. We can, however, understand that God authorizes the permission necessary for wounding experiences to offend us, so that we will be challenged to leave our comfort zones and enter into a new level of maturity in our Christian walk.

If we play the blame game, we merely prolong what must happen anyway. God will continue to probe the conditions of our hearts with various and sundry circumstances until we confront our disguised pride and receive His mercy. When we respond to His provision of grace we receive the capacity to pass through, not park in, even deeper valleys filled with the shadows of death — fearing no evil.

PERSONAL REFLECTION OR DISCUSSION

1. Emotional pain seems to be an integral part of God's plan in bringing us to the place of spiritual maturity. Why do you think there are no shortcuts to maturity?

2. What does the Cross mean to you?

3. How has God "scandalized" you? How have you reacted?

4. Do you see God's love and care for you in the circumstances He has allowed? In what ways?

CHAPTER

- FOURTEEN -

Sirens and Smoke

It is wonderful what God can do with
the broken heart, if He gets all the pieces.
— George Mueller

That blasted phone! In the darkened bedroom I could clearly see the glaring red numbers on the digital clock: 12:43. Moments before, I had been jolted by the cruel sound of the ringing telephone.

In a semi-comatose state I climbed out of my warm bed, struggled with my bathrobe, and then stumbled to the phone. I had no idea how long it had been ringing.

It had been a full day. My pastoral responsibilities had included Saturday morning visitations, hosting a regular radio talk show, studying for Sunday's sermon, and dinner with family and friends. I had been asleep for at least an hour.

"Yes?" I managed groggily after fumbling with the receiver.

"Is this Reverend Freeman?" she inquired in an official sounding tone.

Upon my affirmative reply, she acquainted me with her name and her status as a nurse at the emergency room of a local hospital. "Reverend Freeman," she continued, "I have been instructed to inform you that a family from your church has experienced a fire in their home within the past hour. Are you familiar with the McFarlands?"

"Yes," I responded. My thoughts began to race. I could barely concentrate on her next words.

"At this present time, Vernon and Marge (the parents) are being retained here for a while for smoke inhalation treatment. Larry (the 7 year old) is in critical condition with 95 percent of his body burned. Gordon (11 years old) was burned, but his condition is not known. Both boys are in the ambulance on their way to the Burn Center at Baltimore City Hospital. Vernon and Marge have requested that you go directly to Baltimore City Hospital."

I was dumbfounded. What could I say?

"Any questions?" she added.

"N-No. Thank you," I stammered. "Tell them I'll leave immediately. Thank you. Good-bye."

I put the receiver back into place and felt myself hunching over, with both hands on the kitchen counter — staring blankly at the pattern imprinted in the Formica. I let out a long sigh as the impact of what I had just heard slowly settled into my mind.

Numbly, I walked back to the bedroom. My wife was wide-awake. As I dressed, I explained the situation to her as I had heard it. Moments later I walked outside into the brisk, wintry blast of air.

The 45-minute drive seemed like an eternity with a hundred questions bombarding my mind. Was Larry going to make it? How did the fire start? How badly was Gordon burned? Were Vernon and Marge all right? Was the house completely destroyed? Why did this have to happen to such a fine family? What could I possibly say that would minister to the parents and relatives? Why was I feeling so inadequate?

When I arrived, one of Marge's brothers and his wife were already present in the waiting room. They gave me a sketchy account of the grim situation. Over the next hour, the room began to fill with relatives and close family friends. The burn unit was a beehive of activity as Larry and Gordon were given expert attention.

A while later, the pathetic-looking figures of Vernon and Marge stepped off the elevator. Glazed eyes filled with a mixture of fear and pain. Smudged faces and hands. Winter coats hastily thrown over long johns and pajamas. Not much could be said, so I held them. They wept quietly.

We all found our separate seats and waited for the progress reports on Gordon and Larry. Approximately an hour went by with waves of tears followed by pensive silence. Around 4:30 a.m., the doctor's presence caused everyone to bristle to attention, searching for clues on his worn face. He broke the news gently but firmly. Larry had died. Vernon and Marge desperately clutched each other. They sobbed uncontrollably.

Gordon's condition progressed rapidly with intermittent moments of uncertainty. The days leading up to and following Larry's funeral were challenging for everyone concerned — especially Vernon and Marge.

Listen between the lines as Marge recounts those events that happened nine months ago. I did not dare to retouch the words, afraid that I might spoil their essence. With great respect, I thank her for putting her feelings on paper and then granting permission to share them.

After the fire was under control, fire engines were everywhere. The noise, the stench of fire and water caused an overwhelming urge to vomit. (My memory up to this point is vivid, but I'm just not able to put it on paper.)

Our boys were each in a different ambulance. My husband and I were in a third. Fear. This was the most fearful time in my life. The sound of sirens shook me to the core. This time the sirens were for us. It was my house. My home. My children. I didn't just read it in the paper or know the people somehow. It was me.

In the ambulance, surprisingly, my husband and I were able to talk. Guarding each word, considering the emotional state of the other. We prayed constantly on this 15-minute ride to the hospital. Our prayer and conversation mingled in a very unique way, as we were intensely aware of God's presence. It wasn't necessary to say, "Let's pray." From this time on, my husband and I were united in a brand-new way. At the Cross.

A few days later, sitting across the room from a smaller-than-usual, closed casket, I was gripped with the realization that Larry was a smaller-than-usual person. He just hadn't grown enough to die. Larry was just seven.

He was (to me, anyway) everything a seven year old should be. Cute, happy, ever so kind, not too bright in school, so wonderful to hug and he loved me. He was just a baby. My baby. Larry was supposed to grow up and I was supposed to die first. I was numb, but not too numb.

God sat so close to me on that bench. He had never before been closer. Heaven was so close and real. An attitude of worship totally encompassed me. Almighty God was comforting me.

As I write this, l am weeping. The pain is just as great as ever. The weeks and months spent mourning leave me faint.

Always running to Him like a baby. Daily. Moment by moment. And every single time He's there! Waiting to wipe away my tears as a mother would her son.

When my life fell apart before my eyes, I accused God of not knowing my pain because He was never a mother. I was wrong. Through it all, I learned to call Him "Abba, Father. Daddy."

Suddenly the entire past is equal. Infancy, toddlerhood, kindergarten, and second grade are all the same. The progression of life has stopped. They all were, nothing is. There is no present. There will be no tomorrow.

A very few weeks ago I was at the grocery store. Outside, there were boys eagerly waiting to carry grocery bags. They were so full of life. My heart became physically heavy and I began to sob.

Yelling once again to God, "Larry was

going to do that. He was going to be kind to people and even handsome. It is not fair. He was going to be a fine, young Christian man. Close to You. He was already studying Your Word in school and at home with us."

Well, I've never heard God speak in an audible voice, but His response was perfectly clear — what peace swept over me! I was able to rejoice. God once again had to remind me that He was in control all the time. God's plan was not my plan. God's thoughts were different from my thoughts.

Perhaps that is when I realized that Larry was never truly mine. I was just a steward.

As I look at my new little baby, Jacob, in the infant seat next to me, I see him so fragile, just three months old. I say to him, "You're not mine, either."

Face to face with the sovereignty of God!

Each time I read this account, my eyes well up with tears, knowing that God has specifically comforted each one in this human drama. Some people get bitter when faced with similar trauma. But Vernon and Marge have allowed this trial to tenderize their hearts and make them even sweeter. Life has not been easy for them. At times certain memories will strike without warning and they will weep and then stop as quickly as they began. Both of them have endured dry seasons with spent emotions and emptiness.

Through it all, they have permitted the cross of

Jesus Christ to work out their natural resources and then work in the fruit of the Holy Spirit. Even though they have not consistently felt warm, fuzzy feelings, they have mutually decided to experience God's joy regardless of the circumstances. They have adjusted to God's justice, seeing the loss of their home and the death of their son as an opportunity to view an inexplicable event from His perspective. They have been rewarded with superabundant grace from the hand of God.

It reminds me of the apostle Paul's statement in Philippians 3:8. He said that he had mentally counted everything in his life to be loss. But when he actually suffered the loss of all things, he entered into an advanced phase of maturity that was forced by a series of "unfair" experiences. These terrifying events provided fertilizer with which he could mix the soil of his heart and grow into a new level of fellowship with Jesus Christ in the power of His resurrection so that he, Paul, could rejoice in the midst of even greater suffering.

PERSONAL REFLECTION OR DISCUSSION

1. Through which trials do you think God has sought to increase your patience?

2. Do you agree that a crisis is necessary to apply faith? Why or why not?

3. Do you have the attitude that all you have is owned by God and is merely entrusted to you as a steward? How do you know?

God is a specialist when the anguish is deep. His ability to heal the soul is profound . . . but only those who rely on his wounded Son will experience relief.

(Charles R. Swindoll, 1934–)

FIFTEEN

SKYSCRAPER THEOLOGY

> Sorrow is a fruit; God does not make it
> grow on limbs too weak to bear it.
> — Victor Hugo

See the man over there looking at the blueprint? Go ask him. He'll tell you everything you want to know." Following the pointed finger of the sweaty construction worker, I picked my way carefully through the rocks and dirt. The man with the blueprint looked up with an inquisitive expression. "Son, may I help you?" he asked.

"Oh, yes, sir," I answered. "I don't want to take much of your time, but my curiosity has gotten the best of me. I was hoping you could explain something for my benefit.

"You see, over the past few months I have passed this site a number of times. I've always seen hard-working men all over the place, but nothing seems to be happening. There's no building yet, just a big, gaping hole in the ground and. . . ."

Boy, did he ever take me to school! Before I had a chance to finish, he began to explain some of the intricate details involved in the design and construction of a high-rise building. I must have "uh-huhed" and said, "Oh, I see" about 300 times. He told me how the height of the building determined the width and depth of the concrete footings that went into the ground and also the size and number of the steel reinforcing bars that were placed in the ground before the pouring of the cement.

He showed me the blueprints and related that it had already taken more than two years of planning, drawing, meetings with the zoning board, and the expenditure of thousands of dollars to bring the crew to their current phase of construction. He also stated that the plans for a building this tall forced them to dig down to rock and then pour tons of concrete upon the rock to establish a suitable foundation.

After thanking him for his kindness in educating a willing learner, I returned to my vehicle and drove away with a brand-new respect for those involved in the many stages of a construction industry.

The project I had just visited entailed much advanced planning; site approval; demolition of previous lot coverage; excavation, and the dumping of truckloads of cement; and the strategic placement of steel reinforcement bars. All of this work — and still there were no visible, above-ground results!

Many moons have passed since that episode, yet to this day I cannot get away from an analogy that came to me. What I witnessed and heard at that dusty, noisy construction site is an amazingly accurate story of what happens in all our lives.

So much of the work God does and allows in our lives is unglamorous, employing vast amounts of time with little or no measurable progress. We also find it extremely difficult to understand the reasons why life seems to be treating us so "unfairly."

Stop for a moment and try to imagine yourself as a building. How tall is the building? Is it a 1-story structure? A 10-story edifice? Or maybe a 40 or 50-story skyscraper?

You see, the height determines how deeply God must dig before laying the proper foundation. No human can handle the elevation of God's blessing without the corresponding work of cross-cutting to the core of the soul. God promotes prepared people.

Ask Joseph. He was a skyscraper (Genesis 37–50). As a youngster, he had a dream that, when it was revealed, made him the object of intense hatred and violence from his older brothers. You can imagine him huddling in the bottom of an empty pit in the wilderness or stumbling along as a purchased slave in the dust of an Ishmaelite camel on its way to Egypt. All the while wondering if maybe he had improperly interpreted the dream about the 12 sheaves in the field, the sun, the moon, and the 11 stars. Maybe it didn't mean that this family would bow down before him and make obeisance to him after all.

To make matters worse, upon arrival in Egypt his new master's wife framed him. When Joseph refused to be sexually seduced by her, it looked like he was preparing for a career in prison. Things looked grim and they also looked "unfair." But God was only excavating the dirt for a firm foundation for this skyscraper.

Before all was said and done, Joseph became governor over all the land of Egypt and was used mightily by God to help thousands of people during a severe famine. Years passed and his dream was fulfilled. Joseph could then proclaim to his brothers, "You plotted evil against me, but God turned it into good, in order to preserve the lives of many people who are alive today because of what happened" (see Gen. 50:20). God promotes people who will allow Him to prepare the soil of their hearts for solid foundations.

But how does God prepare us? My friend, it is in the school of suffering. I wish there were some other easier answer. Afflictions that come in the form of uncontrollable events or nasty, critical people are some of the trials God uses to dig away the dirt and get down to the bedrock. During these times, it hurts deeply. The pain is unbearable.

In the meantime, Satan isn't sleeping. He portrays pain as illogical, unreasonable, and "unfair." He desires for us to remain as one-story people with tiny, one-story capacities for the foundational riches discovered in God's Word, the Bible. Satan also tries to cause us to harbor mental-attitude sins of jealousy and envy toward Christians who are growing in their walk with the Lord.

While God is using circumstances to dig and blast in preparation for the foundation, there seems to be no spiritual progress. No visible results appear above the surface. In fact, our mental, emotional, and spiritual lives actually seem to be in confusion and upheaval. It is during these times, however, that we need to take heart, to encourage ourselves in the Lord and refuse to faint. We must fortify ourselves with the lively hope that benefits us with maturity in time and rewards in eternity.

The choice is up to you. God will not violate your freedom of choice. Do you want to be a normal, one-story person with a shallow foundation and convenient, comfortable, predictable Christianity that gets tossed to and fro with every storm? Or do you want to be a skyscraper person who bleeds every situation for every bit of maturity you can squeeze from it? How about it? Just dutifully existing in life, or attacking it with unbridled enthusiasm?

You may be saying, "But my foundation has already been laid and the building program in my life is in its advanced stages. Recently, the zoning board of heaven ruled that any further construction would present serious potential damage to my family, my neighbors, and myself. They based their ruling on the sub-standard material I chose and the shortcuts I employed with planning and building my life. In other words, my life doesn't meet the universal regulations of God's building code. What am I to do?"

You have two options:

1. Ignore the warning. Keep on building. Attain new, precarious heights of success and prosperity. Eat, drink, and be merry. Enjoy life for the present flush of excitement and entertainment. Run with the in-crowd. Avoid spiritual principles at all cost. They might make you uncomfortable and make you think about the consequences of your avoidance mentality and behavior.

2. Heed the warning. Stop construction. Separate who you are from the plans you used. Walk in humility before God while He uses the Word, His precious Holy Spirit, and possibly some "unfair" circumstances to assist in demolishing the old so He can establish the new. God will use His blueprints, His building material, and His construction techniques. It will be worth the honesty and the pain.

PERSONAL REFLECTION OR DISCUSSION

1. In what ways do you identify with Joseph?

2. Think back on a time when you had no visible results of maturity evident in your life. How did you trust God during that time of self-doubt?

3. God promotes prepared people. Meditate on this truth and apply it to your life today.

4. Name a challenge you are facing today. Plan to face it head-on rather than run from it.

CHAPTER

- SIXTEEN -

GRIEF IN MANY LANGUAGES

> To have suffered much is like knowing
> many languages. It gives the sufferer access
> to many more people.   — Anonymous

Have you ever been stuck in the airport of a foreign country? And then 20 taxi drivers descended upon you? Did you try to haggle with them in your "I-am-a-bilingually-illiterate-helpless-tourist" mode? Factor in the existing language or dialect barrier and you have an exhilarating experience on your hands. Yeah, right.

There's no question that since the confusion at the Tower of Babel, the different cultures and languages have presented many fascinating challenges.

A few years ago I met Marie, a pleasant woman in her late twenties, who put another spin to all this. While still in her teen years, Marie discovered that she had cancer in her leg. It was quite a shock to this vivacious, athletic girl. She, her family, and her close friends rode the roller coaster of emotions, ranging from despair to hope, for a couple of years.

Finally it became apparent that the doctors were going to have to amputate just above the knee in order to spare her life. What happened next was an intriguing study in human nature.

Her father, a high-profile pastor, got real mad at God. It was no secret. He thought that the whole situation was terribly "unfair." Well, some of the more vocal church members took him to task. "You, of all people," they said, "should know better. You should trust God and realize that He has everything under control. Stop being angry and start trusting."

Marie, on the other hand seemed to express nothing but curiosity about her situation. Yes, curiosity. Her emotional state of curiosity encompassed several areas. Am I going to be able to play field hockey again? If so, how well? How weird is the prosthetic device going to look? When I am sitting with my legs crossed and with my fake leg sticking out, are people going to stare at me? Will I be able to run and jump? She was intrigued about her response to the loss of her leg.

Interestingly enough, some of the same people at church took a different tack with her. "Maybe you are in denial, Marie. You need to feel and express your anger more openly. C'mon, let it out. Don't push it down."

As Marie related the whole scenario to me, a deeper understanding about the nature of grief began to emerge: We all grieve, but we grieve in different languages. Just as Marie and her father grieved in different ways, your grief language will probably be different from the manner in which others grieve. Perhaps this is a significant part of the reason why some people make such insensitive, bordering-on-cruel remarks to those found in the arena of emotional pain.

God made us and He understands our capacity for grief and also our need to express the same. When Moses died at the ripe old age of 120, the people of Israel responded in a very natural way. Deuteronomy 34:8 records that the nation wept and mourned over the loss for 30 days.

God didn't say, "Oy vey. Enough already. Stop grieving. Don't you know that Moses is here in paradise with me? He is much better off. If you had the big picture, you'd stop your crying."

Instead, true to His merciful nature, God permitted them to grieve. And then when the grief work was completed, it was time for them to move on under Joshua's leadership. They were now in the position to apprehend, with vibrant hope, what had been promised to them in Canaan.

Grief, whether it is big or little, past or present, is sponsored by loss. Thousands of years ago, the Israelite nation grieved over the loss of Moses' leadership. As we fast-forward a few thousand years, we meet Marie who has lost a functioning limb. Her father's loss was very emotional regarding the dreams and aspirations he had for his daughter.

What kind of loss have you encountered? A job? A special friend? A failure in school? Physical movement? A marriage? A body part? The freedom of singleness? A shattered dream? Valuable years that have been frittered away?

Next question. What language do you grieve in? Do you behave in a manner that you are not proud of? Do you stomp around in a blustery, intimidating manner? Do you have a vindictive nature that tends toward bitterness and exacting retribution on anyone who has

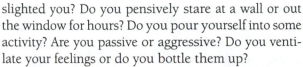

slighted you? Do you pensively stare at a wall or out the window for hours? Do you pour yourself into some activity? Are you passive or aggressive? Do you ventilate your feelings or do you bottle them up?

Whatever your grief language is, grieve, and grieve boldly. The emotions come in like a tidal wave. Anger. Tears. Laughter. Guilt. Grab your surfboard and ride the wave in your grief language . . . in the way that you do it. Not the way you have read or were told it should be done.

When you have been through personal heartache, some people will feel compelled to say something to you about your particular situation. In their awkwardness, they may blurt out irrelevant observations. Others will be drawn to you, thinking you are some kind of "guru." They will pour out their problems to you and may chide you if you have no magical formulas for them. Don't feel pressured by their expectations of you. They are attracted to you because they want to tap into the invisible support system that has enabled you to function during your trials. Whether you like it or not, they probably consider you an expert in knowing how to handle tough times. If you have a word of wisdom for them, share it. If you have nothing specific to communicate to them, admit it with confidence and offer your friendship and prayers.

In the Chinese language the character for crisis is made up of two words: opportunity and danger. And that's part of what happens when we grieve. This book is about looking for the opportunity that is present in every crisis.

But there is also danger. Suffering provides an environment whereby individuals may say things, think things, or make choices that go against their theology. Many are shocked to discover some of the evil, dark stuff that gurgles in the cauldrons of their hearts. There is the tendency, however, to forget that we serve an unshakable God who already knows that. Under the thin veneer of our cultured carnality lies danger. There is a fine line that runs between danger and opportunity. We all have to walk it. It's a slippery slope. It is called the grieving process.

Granger Westberg, in his book *Good Grief*, describes this normal process through which most of us must go as we face up to the losses in our lives. Before getting back into the main stream of life, grief-struck people usually pass through the following stages in their own language:

1. State of shock (temporary anesthesia).
2. Emotion is expressed (grieving openly).
3. Depressed and lonely feelings (God doesn't care).
4. Physical symptoms of distress (psychosomatic problems).
5. Panic.
6. Sense of guilt (neurotic).
7. Hostility and resentment (cynical toward God and friends).
8. Unable to re-enter usual activities (can't grieve in presence of others).
9. Gradual hope (darkness begins to break up).
10. Affirm reality (continual growth).[1]

The process of grief is as predictable as the law of gravity. The way each person charts his or her way through the grief process is not quite as predictable. A giant tsunami wave of heartache strikes and then recedes as quickly as it came. You're laughing. And then you're sobbing uncontrollably. A few minutes pass and then you're okay. Why ask why? That's just the way it is. You are not going insane.

Certain songs on the radio, certain restaurants, and certain memories all form a conspiracy, haunting one with thoughts of a happier time. The quiet, gnawing pain seems to be there under the surface — always present.

What about anticipatory grief? For years in advance, the grieving process slowly hits the friends and relatives of someone who is suffering from a debilitating disease like cancer. When the person dies, everyone has already walked through a significant amount of the grief. That is why the spouse of someone in a similar situation will sometimes remarry within a year or so after the spouses' death. Others are shocked and upset. But others will never really know how much that spouse has been grieving for years.

Even when surrounded by some dear, well-meaning friends, the grieving process is a very lonely task. Like Lily Tomlin once stated, "We're all in this alone." No one else can weep, get angry, or for that matter, go crazy for you in your stead. You are the one who must resist the icy grip of bitterness, the seductive whisper of suicide, the strangled screams of fear. And you will.

In 1997 I co-wrote the book *Return To Glory: The Powerful Stirring of the African-American Man*. For this book I interviewed 40-50 black men, discovering that there is an inseparable link between racism and the grieving process. How does a young man or young lady of six years of age come to grips with the cruel reality that the rules of society are somehow different for them just because of the color of their skin? I came to understand that loss and grief come in many forms.

In the midst of suffering, regardless of what sponsors it, we learn to turn our thoughts to what is clear and certain about God, rather than to what He has chosen to conceal. Suffering helps us realize our radical dependence upon the One who can, but sometimes won't.

PERSONAL REFLECTION OR DISCUSSION

1. Think about a recent loss. What were some of the feelings and thoughts you encountered? How have you worked through the grief process?

2. What is your grief language?

3. Select three people. Encourage them this week, either by a telephone call, a personal visit, or a note.

CHAPTER

- SEVENTEEN -

GOD CAN, BUT SOMETIMES WON'T

A full and complete reading of the New Testament will show conclusively that God has not promised to solve our problems or answer our questions or melt away our tribulations. If we can ever get our sense of values in proper Christian focus, we will come to understand that the loving presence of God in the trial furnace is a far greater blessing than the elimination of trouble by divine intervention.

— Erwin G. Tieman

Omnipotence. Aren't you impressed with the way I started off the final chapter of this book with such a fancyshmancy word? If you're not, I still won't let you spoil it for me — I'm impressed!

Question: What does this noble, awe-inspiring word mean? Answer: God is all-powerful. Period. He can do anything. He can heal all diseases and empty all hospital wards. He can eradicate all crime and stop the abuse of all innocent victims. He can extinguish all wars and squash out all injustice. He can bring harmony to all people and feed all hungry stomachs. He can alleviate all problems that cause mortal agony and eliminate physical death. Get the picture? He can do everything. No, ifs, ands, or buts. He has all power.

We must understand that God's omnipotence is never in question when it comes to freedom from suffering. There is no crisis from which there is no deliverance, since deliverance can come through life or through physical death. Rather, liberation from pain and trauma is a question of His sovereignty.

Question: Okay now, what does this magnificent word, sovereignty, mean? Answer: God will do anything He wants to do, bound only by His own character. In other words, if freedom from a situation that produces pain is a part of His master plan, the individual will be rescued; if not, God has another purpose for the life of the person that is guaranteed to bring Him the most glory. Period.

If He wants to deliver Daniel from the salivating jaws of hungry lions, or let James get decapitated, or let Peter experience an angelic escort from prison, or permit thousands of Christians to get martyred in Roman coliseums, or to allow His only Son, Jesus, to suffer the cruel death of crucifixion to satisfy His justice, He will.

Jonathan understands this principle. He has learned it the hard way. His 18-year-old eyes communicate mischief as he tries to run over my toes with his souped-up electric wheelchair. (Remind me to wear my steel-toed boots next time I visit him.)

Four years ago Jonathan was riding his ten-speed bicycle when a drunken driver careened across the median strip and hit him broadside. Jonathan pitched head over heels for 30 yards. The next thing he remembered was the soft touch of a nurse's hand on his forehead — five days later.

As a paraplegic, Jonathan has battled the icy grip of self-pity. He's grappled with the seductive whisper of suicide. But you know what? He has won a tremendous victory — he has accepted God's sovereignty in the whole matter.

Jonathan's physical condition has made marginal improvements. His attitude, however, has made a 180-degree turn, from cyclical bouts with rage and hopelessness to sparkling eyes filled with an eternal purpose for living. He has become a "wounded healer," comforting others wherein he has been comforted.

I have joined many others in praying for Jonathan's healing. Remember, God's omnipotence reveals that He can instantly heal even a young man required by the facts of medical science to spend the rest of his days in a wheelchair. But God's omnipotence is not in question. The real issue is His sovereignty.

Will God get more glory out of a miraculous healing that baffles the doctors with their x-rays and empirical data? Or will He obtain more glory from Jonathan's pure testimony of His faithfulness and love in spite of the heartache of his predicament? Only God knows. And He does.

We pray in faith, believing for Jonathan's healing, knowing full well that God can do anything. At the same time, we submit our request to God's sovereignty. We also pray that God will strengthen Jonathan's inner-soul capacity, trusting that he will cling fiercely to God's promises and not focus on the questions of "fairness."

Either way provides the opportunity to give God all the glory and honor; supernatural physical healing or personal response to His equally supernatural provision of patience and trust. It is a double-win situation. This principle holds true in every circumstance that happens to us, whether good or bad, "fair" or "unfair."

Meanwhile, Jonathan is content. He has joined Chuck Swindoll in claiming these two truths that come from the book *Improving Your Serve*:

1. Nothing touches me that has not passed through the hands of my Heavenly Father. Nothing.
2. Everything I endure is designed to prepare me for serving others more effectively. Everything.[1]

Jonathan refuses to let anything or anyone rob him of his joy. In fact, his passion for playing practical jokes and tricks on unsuspecting victims almost borders on terrorist activity. "Ouch! There he goes again — over my toes!"

Submitting to God's sovereignty keeps us in the position of humble servants who are available, with tender hearts to serve Him regardless of the uncontrollable, life-changing events that help determine our lot in life. We choose to draw our water from the well that never runs dry. We studiously avoid the satanic snares of trying to evaluate the "fairness" of our particular set of circumstances and comparing our lives with those of others.

Any approach other than that of yielding to His sovereignty leaves us high and dry. Either we drown in a pool of rationalized self-pity or we become little monsters demanding that God serve us at our bidding. Of course, these mutes cause us to forfeit the privilege of seeing the fourth man in the furnace and cause us to relinquish the joy of seeing hungry lions get their mouths shut. We go through life being pulled by our own ego needs, wants, and demands.

God knows our true need. For some of us, the need is for one or more inexplicable, earth-shaking situation(s) that captures our attention and causes us to focus on eternal values like never before. For others, the need may be different. We may not pass through such intense encounters with pain. Oh yes, we hurt at times and it is the same type of pain, but the outward circumstances may be less dramatic.

God can deliver, but sometimes he won't. Why? Because He is working all things together for His purpose. And our response? Trust. Humble, child-like trust.

Is God "fair"? No, not from our limited, earthly perspective. But is He just and merciful? Absolutely.

Remember, we are just passing through this period of "child-training" here on earth.

While we continue to be responsible with our daily tasks, let's keep our eyes upon the glory of the hereafter regardless of the seeming "unfairness" of God in the present. God is not "fair." He is just! Period.

Fleas notwithstanding.

Humble yourselves, therefore, under God's mighty hand, that He may lift you up in due time. Cast all your anxiety on him because he cares for you.

Be self-controlled and alert. Your enemy the devil prowls around like a roaring lion looking for someone to devour. Resist him, standing firm in the faith, because you know that your brothers throughout the world are undergoing the same kind of suffering.

And the God of all grace, who called you to his eternal glory in Christ, after you have suffered a little while, will himself restore you and make you strong, firm, and steadfast. To him be the power forever and ever. Amen (1 Pet. 5:6–11; NIV).

PERSONAL REFLECTION OR DISCUSSION

1. What does God's sovereignty mean to you?

2. List three fears you have about the future. After each, write these words: GOD IS IN CONTROL.

3. If you have the assurance that God has a plan for your life, you will see all that comes into your life as the outworking of His grand design. Remember, He is the master weaver, and we see the tapestry of life as seemingly tangled threads from the reverse side. He sees the beautiful pattern He is working in and through us.

ENDNOTES

Chapter 2

1 Paul Malte, *Why Does God Allow Suffering?* (St. Louis, MO: Lutheran Laymen's League, 1965), p. 5.

Chapter 3

1 Anton Szandor LaVey, *The Satanic Bible* (New York, NY: Avon Books, 1969), p. 30–35.

2 Mick Jagger and Keith Richards, "Sympathy for the Devil," copyright 1968, ABKCO Music, New York City, NY 10019. Used by permission.

Chapter 5

1 W.E. Vine, *An Expository Dictionary of New Testament Words* (Old Tappan, NJ: Fleming H. Revell Company, 1981), p. 55–56.

2 Ibid.

Chapter 13

1 Ibid., p. 130.

2 Josh McDowell, *More Than a Carpenter* (Wheaton, IL: Living Books, 1977), p. 61.

3 Peter Kreeft, *Making Sense Out of Suffering* (Ann Arbor, MI: Servant Books, 1986), p. 125–126.

Chapter 16

1 Granger Westberg, *Good Grief* (Philadelphia, PA: Fortress Press, 1961), p. 11–50.

Chapter 17

1 Charles R. Swindoll, *Improving Your Serve* (Waco, TX: Word Books, 1981), p. 189.

Joel A. Freeman

Joel A. Freeman, Ph.D., author of four other internationally acclaimed books, holds a Master of Science degree in counseling from Loyola College (Baltimore) and also holds a Ph.D. in the same discipline. Listed in Marquis' *Who's Who in the World*, he served as mentor/chaplain for the NBA Washington Bullets/Wizards (1979–1998). As president of The Freeman Institute consulting firm, Dr. Freeman facilitates team building/leadership/change management/diversity initiatives for leaders of other nations, government agencies, corporations and faith-based organizations. Joel, Shirley, and family reside in Maryland.

www.freemaninstitute.com
joel@freemaninstitute.com